# VOICELESS CUSTOMER

# VOICELESS CUSTOMER

## WHY CUSTOMERS LEAVE

### DR. FABIOLA CORVERA-STIMELING

COCENTRUM
PUBLISHING

Publisher's Cataloging-In-Publication Data

(Prepared by The Donohue Group, Inc.)

Names: Corvera-Stimeling, Fabiola.

Title: Voiceless customer : why customers leave / Dr. Fabiola Corvera-Stimeling.

Description: Anthem, Arizona : Cocentrum Publishing, [2017] | Includes bibliographical references and index.

Identifiers: LCCN 2017939418 | ISBN 978-0-9989063-0-0 (hardcover) | ISBN 978-0-9989063-1-7 (paperback) | ISBN 978-0-9989063-2-4 (ebook)

Subjects: LCSH: Customer relations. | Relationship marketing. | Customer loyalty. | Service industries. | Success in business.

Classification: LCC HF5415.5 .C67 2017 (print) | LCC HF5415.5 (ebook) | DDC 658.8/12–dc23

*To my parents who made every sacrifice to give me what they did not have.*

*To my husband who has made every dream possible from the day we started sharing a life together.*

# CONTENTS

# INTRODUCTION

The goal of *Voiceless Customer: Why Customers Leave* is to help service companies understand how they can better serve and retain their customers. Customer experience has become a hot business topic, but business decision-makers lack the knowledge to create a clear strategy. This book is a guide for managers, directors, executives, and business owners looking to improve their customers' experiences, enabling them to retain more customers. The customer lens offers a non-corporate view of some of the problems service organizations, like yours, are facing as well as strategies for addressing these problems.

Organizations must respond to market and customer demands. Business leaders recognize the importance of customer-focused operations as a competitive advantage (McCall, 2016). Under-spending on customer retention efforts will have a greater detrimental effect on long-term customer profitability than under-spending on customer acquisition (Reinartz et al., 2005). Companies are finding it necessary to move away from a company-centric approach to a more customer-centric approach (Bettencourt et al., 2014). Customers expect to be part of the service process;

in fact, they expect every company to fulfill their individual demands. Unfortunately, this is a challenging task, and most organizations fall short in their attempts to meet their customers' needs. There is a vast misunderstanding of what it takes for a company to better serve its customers. Over the long term, ignoring customers' demands will be detrimental to the sustainability of the business.

The service industry is the fastest-growing industry worldwide. It comprises approximately 63% of the nominal gross domestic product (GDP) in the world (Central Intelligence Agency, n.d.) and approximately 80% ($9.81 trillion) of the US private-sector GDP (Ward, 2010). As the service industry overtakes the manufacturing industry, companies have begun to transition from a product-view to a solution-view perspective (Schettkat & Yocarini, 2006). However, this extraordinary service industry growth has not been accompanied by a focus on fulfilling customer expectations. Customer retention has not been a top priority for business owners despite the positive impact it has on company profits (Jao, 2015). Firms cannot continue to focus only on competing through providing excellent services. Instead, companies should move into managing the customer experience through the co-creation of memorable experiences (Bitner et al., 2008).

For years, I have studied service organizations, particularly mature service organizations, which face the biggest challenges in customer retention due to their silo and segmented structures. Some of the customer experience solutions currently available are high-level ideas, leaving executives with no specific guidance on how to implement them. Some companies have become almost paralyzed when addressing customer needs. They have failed to deliver what the customer currently wants and to predict what the customer will need in the future. This lack of guidance leaves companies with little direction and few recommendations to help them improve their customers' experiences and customer retention.

Before addressing customer experience, we need to understand value co-creation. Value co-creation is a process through which the interactions of a company and its customers facilitate the creation of value (Grönroos & Voima, 2013; Ramesh et al., 2012). Value is co-created only through interactions between the customer and the firm, and only customers can perceive and determine value in a service transaction (Vargo & Lusch, 2004b; Vargo et al., 2008). This collaborative experience becomes the basis of value (Prahalad & Ramaswamy, 2004b), which is why it is necessary to explain value co-creation before discussing customer experience. An understanding of value co-creation allows us to discern why some companies are great at servicing and retaining their customers while others are not.

Some companies who are struggling to fulfill their customer needs fall prey to losing focus on the customer instead of committing their efforts and resources to identifying and solving the real cause of their customer retention difficulties. These organizations may focus more on new customer acquisition efforts to compensate for their customer attrition. Studies have demonstrated the importance of customer retention; for example, the cost of acquiring a new customer is anywhere from 5 to 25 times higher than the cost to retain an existing one (Gallo, 2014). Studies have also revealed that increasing customer retention by 5% increases profits between 25% and 95% (Gallo, 2014). According to the 2014 American Express Global Customer Service Barometer (American Express, 2014), 74% of surveyed consumers have spent more with a company due to a history of positive customer service experiences, and over one-third of surveyed consumers would switch companies due to a poor service experience. Customer retention cannot be the responsibility of one department (e.g. marketing); rather, it should be a collaborative effort between the company, customers, and vendors that lies at the center of the company's innovation strategy.

Customers determine the level of service they expect from the companies with which they do business, and they demand the same level of service from every company. They do not distinguish between their online retailer, restaurant, doctor, or coffee shop. Demand for a better experience will not only continue, but it will increase because Millennials expect outstanding customer experiences any time they interact with a company (Barbera, 2015). This is now the largest generation in the United States, representing one-quarter of the nation's population (United States Census Bureau, 2015). Millennials are also the most educated and diverse generation in the history of the United States (Barbera, 2015). They are tech-savvy and well-informed. Therefore, focusing on improving how companies fulfill customer needs will continue to not only remain relevant, but also drive their long-term strategy.

I titled this book *Voiceless Customer: Why Customers Leave* because few companies stand behind the services they offer, leaving customers without support when they encounter an issue. In my research, I have identified three types of companies: companies that listen to their customers, but do not know how to fix the problem; companies that listen to their customers and work hard to fix the problem; and companies that choose to ignore their customers. If you fall into the first category, this book is for you. I will provide you with knowledge you can use to improve your customers' experiences and your company's customer retention strategy every day. If you fall into the second category, you are one of the few companies with a successful customer retention strategy, and we need to learn from you and follow your example. If you fall into the third category, I'd be surprised to learn you'd taken the time to read this book.

If you are ready to get started, *Voiceless Customer: Why Customers Leave* will provide you a clear path detailing what you need to do to make the necessary changes to address the core of the customer retention problems inside your organization. This book shows you "how" rather than just telling you "what" is necessary to retain your customers. A framework is presented to help you through this journey to fulfill customer needs and transform your business into a sustainable one through constant innovation and collaboration with your customers.

Enjoy!

# CHAPTER 1

## OVERALL IMPACT OF NOT FULFILLING CUSTOMER NEEDS

*"A customer is the most important visitor on our premises, he is not dependent on us. We are dependent on him. He is not an interruption in our work. He is the purpose of it. He is not an outsider in our business. He is part of it. We are not doing him a favor by serving him. He is doing us a favor by giving us an opportunity to do so." – Mahatma Gandhi*

Failing to fulfill customer needs due to poor customer service is costing businesses billions per year. Companies across the globe are struggling to meet customer expectations, which makes it extremely hard to retain their customers. In the US alone, poor customer service is costing businesses $62 billion per year (Hyken, 2016). UK companies are losing £37 billion per year due to bad customer service (Colson, 2017). In Australia, poor customer experience is costing that nation's businesses AU$122 billion a year (Writers, 2016).

The service industry is driven by customer demands, and customer experience is becoming the primary basis for competition (McCall, 2016). Customers expect simplicity, ease, and common sense from the companies they do business with. For most service organizations, providing simplicity and ease of doing business is where they fall short. We are living in a service-oriented economy, but customer satisfaction is no higher than it was in 1970 (Consumer Reports, 2015). Some studies report that customer service is actually getting worse instead of getting better (Cameron, 2016; Swinscoe, 2015). Developments in information technology have transformed the manner in which customers experience a service encounter and their relationship with a service provider (Scherer et al., 2015).

Customer expectations are increasing, and firms are struggling to fulfill their customers' demands. Customers' patience when dealing with a problem is limited. We cannot blame them when a high percentage of customers' inquiries are ignored and they cannot find a solution at the first point of contact with their service provider. Typically, it takes four or more attempts with the company before their problem is resolved (Grainer et al., 2014).

Because we live in a dynamic environment, customers do not have time to waste. When customers experience a problem with a service firm, the majority will not express their sentiment and will just move their business elsewhere. More than two-thirds of dissatisfied customers do not contact the offending firm to complain (Marketing, 2006; Stephens & Gwinner, 1998). Customer retention becomes even more challenging when looking at it across generations. Millennials are 67% more likely to switch to another company, while only 27% of Baby-Boomers will do so (Hyken, 2016). When it comes to customers, service firms should not follow the old adage that no news is good news. For companies who do not engage with their customers, taking their customers' pulse becomes a challenging task. Mature service organizations experience the greatest challenge to adjust their business model to better serve their customers. In most cases, their service delivery framework prevents them from making the rapid changes necessary to collaborate and engage with their customers.

Advancement in information technology has not necessarily translated into an improved experience for customers. Digital platforms have provided additional outlets for customers to find resolutions to their service issues. Unfortunately, only 21% of customers reported having consistently received an answer to their complaint (American Express, 2014), which means that 79% of customers have been ignored. Some companies may be listening to their clients, but they may not know how to fix the problem. Service organizations face internal challenges that create barriers, which prevent them from becoming more proactive and fulfilling current and future customer demands. Instead, they become reactive, making it difficult for companies to focus on the customer and find ways to innovate. In fact, 80% of organizations think they deliver an outstanding customer experience while only 8% of customers agree with this statement (Allen et al., 2015).

Understanding customer needs is a complex process, and customers often experience difficulty explaining their needs and wants in regard to a service (Thomke & von Hippel, 2002). That is why simply listening to customers is no longer a viable framework to innovate. Service firms cannot act independently (Prahalad & Ramaswamy, 2004a); instead, they need to collaborate with their customers to design services that improve customer experience and simplify service delivery (D'Emidio et al., 2014). Companies that have been able to make value co-creation the center of their business model outperform the competition in terms of revenue growth, profit margins, capital efficiency, and enterprise value (Libert et al., 2015).

A research study found that companies tend to focus more than 80% of their time on primarily having customers recommend their company to others, rather than encouraging customers to collaborate and participate in the value-creation process (Merlo et al., 2014). Some of the reasons provided in this study reflected the lack of framework, platforms, and knowledge on how to effectively collaborate with customers (Merlo et al., 2014). The service industry will continue to be disrupted as technology advances and companies innovate through value co-creation (Corvera-Stimeling, 2015). Service innovation is driven by the desire to fulfill customer needs. Companies who provide customers a simple way of doing business have been able to disrupt an entire sector of the service industry. The insurance, travel, bank, legal, retail, health, fitness, education, car, hospitality, and entertainment industries all have been disrupted by customer-driven services. In this environment, mature companies with departmental silos and legacy systems will continue to struggle at fulfilling customer needs.

Until the customer becomes the focal point of innovation efforts, gaps will remain between what customers want and what service organizations are delivering. We have transitioned from the goods or product-view focus to the service or solution-view perspective. Product innovation and service innovation are not the same. In the following section, I offer a brief overview of the service industry and highlight the differences between the service and product industries.

# CHAPTER 2

## WHAT IS SERVICE?

*"People don't want to buy a quarter-inch drill. They want a quarter-inch hole!" – Theodore Levitt*

Service is what is always exchanged, and goods serve as the distribution of that service (Lusch et al., 2010). While product innovation and service innovation are different, most of our current understanding in service innovation comes from the product-innovation industry (Chae, 2014). Two major differences between product and service innovation are that a service cannot be stored or inventoried like a product, and a service is produced and consumed at the same time, while a product is manufactured first and then consumed (Nijssen et al., 2006;

Tatikonda & Zeithaml, 2002). These differences are highly important when trying to understand service innovation. Your company might manufacture a product that serves as the vehicle or platform for how a service is delivered.

Let me provide you with an example. I have been a customer of German cars for several years. I buy them because they give me peace of mind. Knowing that my family and I are safe makes any trip extremely enjoyable. I know that, if I have a problem with the car, the company will stand behind their product. All the reasons I just mentioned go beyond the actual product. When I purchase a car, I tend to buy the extra services they provide: maintenance, tire protection, and roadside assistance. Why? Because all these ancillary services help me fulfill my needs—the car serves as the vehicle to distribute this service. As a customer, I do not consider purchasing a car simply because I want a car. I purchase the car because it offers me a safe ride and makes me feel protected. I choose a car that gives me some confidence that, if I have a problem with the vehicle, the company is going to stand behind it and make it right for me as the customer.

Products are considered resources on which an operation is performed to produce an effect (Vargo & Lusch, 2004a). Failing to recognize products as a resource to facilitate a service will create shortfalls when analyzing the whole service-delivery system. Service is not an alternative form of product (Vargo & Lusch, 2004a). In my previous example, the car is the safest car on the market, making it arguably the best product. However, it is not simply a product; it is a distribution mechanism of a service. In this arena, the company is falling short at delivering what the customer needs.

After I bought the car, I was a satisfied customer until I took my car for its 3,000-mile service. I made an appointment to drop my car off, but when I arrived at the dealer, no one was there. I had to park my car to try to find someone. I walked inside the service area where I told the receptionist that I had an appointment at 9:00 a.m. and I was not sure why my service rep was not waiting for me.

She said, "It is cold outside, so the service reps are inside waiting for their appointments. Let me call your service rep, and he will meet you outside.'"

I was starting to get annoyed. The service rep met me outside and asked if I wanted to wait for my car because it was going to be only a few hours. The dealer offered coffee and snacks, so I decided to spend my time in the waiting area. I was in line when I noticed that only service technicians were in front of me, waiting to get coffee. My irritation grew because, after waiting for my service rep, I now had to wait in line because the service technicians that work on the cars were getting coffee. What is wrong with this story from a customer perspective? In my mind, the company cares for their employees, which is good, but they have forgotten to take care of the customer.

The story gets better, so please stay with me. As I mentioned, I had arrived for my appointment around 9:00 a.m. After I waited for more than two hours, I went to the customer service desk to check the status on my car. The customer service representative told me that the service rep who was working on my car had gone for lunch, so I had to wait for him to come back. At that point, I was furious because, once again, the company failed to consider the customer in their service delivery.

It is important to recognize that products serve as the mechanism for delivering a service (Lusch et al., 2010). The German carmaker is not a product company; rather, the vehicle is the distribution platform of a service. It is apparent there is a gap in the service delivery for this German car manufacturer. As a loyal customer, I complained to their service manager. Unfortunately, my voice was not heard as I experienced similar issues from a service perspective at my next three visits to this service facility.

My argument here is not to undervalue this German company, but to exemplify the damage a company can do to their brand when failing to recognize how to fulfill customer needs and identify ways to continue innovating. Success requires more than just designing the most amazing driving machine; rather, the business must also understand how all the internal and external stakeholders involved in their service-delivery model are performing when it comes to creating value for their customers. In the German car company example, the car dealer plays a crucial role in this cycle. The dealer and all departments involved in the service delivery—sales, finance, service, and maintenance—are the face of the German company in the customers' eyes. Customers don't deal with the company headquarters back in Germany or the engineers who designed the vehicle. In this example, from the customer's perspective, the German company failed to fulfill this customer's needs. I have dealt with four different dealers; on all four occasions, the experience was the same.

This German car company is not the only company experiencing this problem. Most mature service organizations are struggling to integrate all their fragmented systems and platforms to create a more unified view of the customer to better serve and retain their customers (Rai & Sambamurthy, 2006). Mature service organizations face a bigger challenge than smaller service organizations. I am not minimizing the challenges newer service organizations have, but the nature of being new allows them to be more agile and nimble to make the necessary changes needed to co-create value with their customers. Even so, newer companies are also falling short when fulfilling customer needs. So, what are these companies missing?

You are probably asking yourself: Is my company making the same mistakes these companies are making? Is my company fulfilling customer needs? Is my company involving our customers to modify existing services and design new ones? The service-delivery model for every organization is different. Some of these service models involve several parties, including external partners or vendors, who are involved in fulfilling customer needs and impacting the outcome of the customer experience. The customer sees every department as one company. If I buy a car from the dealer, take the car for service, and receive a loaner vehicle while my car is in service, all the players involved in this service exchange are one company in my eyes: the German car manufacturer. The customer does not understand that the sales department is not aware of what happens with the service department or that the company that handles the loaner vehicles is actually a third-party vendor. For the customer, every single interaction is part of one. The problem some companies are experiencing is that, due to their structure, they are forgetting the most important element of their service-delivery model: the customer. For this reason, as a business decision-maker for your organization, you need to start looking at the problem with a customer lens.

# CHAPTER 3

---

## THE ROLE OF INFORMATION TECHNOLOGY IN THE SERVICE INDUSTRY

*"The human spirit must prevail over technology." – Albert Einstein*

Information technology (IT) has transformed the ways in which customers interact with service organizations (Chae, 2014). Service organizations that have been effective in service innovation have been able to collaborate with their customers by designing services to improve customer experience and by simplifying service delivery (D'Emidio et al., 2014). For several organizations, collaboration with their customers is non-existent or sporadic with no processes in place to put this structure to work. Organizations need to transform their service-delivery framework to be able to collaborate with their customers, and this is where most of the efforts to improve customer experience fall short.

Unfortunately, there is limited information on how a service organization can transform into a nimble and agile organization capable of cooperating with their customers to facilitate service innovation. Advances in technology have allowed companies to compete by facilitating access to a global knowledge network including suppliers, manufacturers, partners, and customers (Prahalad & Ramaswamy, 2004b). Service-delivery models have become more complex, and the customer in some cases has been removed from the model and portrayed as an external beneficiary of the service. Service models like the one I just described assume that the service created by internal members is the service the customer wants. The customer is invited to this exchange at the end of the process, where organizations expect the customer to be excited about this service that was created just for them.

But, wait a second: if it was created just for them, where was the customer throughout this process? Let me give you another example. Last year, I was looking to reduce the amount of electricity and water I spent while washing and drying clothes, but I also wanted units that were really quiet. I decided to purchase a new top-load washer and dryer. I did some research, which included reading customer reviews online, and the feedback was mostly positive. So, I went ahead and invested almost $2,000 in a washer and dryer, and I purchased the company's five-year protection plan. For the first two months, the units performed as expected. Then one day, the dryer started making a horrible grinding noise. I called the store where I bought the units, and I got lost in the automated self-service call system. Finally, I was able to reach a call center rep. I explained the problem, and he told me he was going to transfer me to the actual manufacturer. Again, I waited, and once someone answered the call, I had to explain again why I was calling. After I described my problem, the call representative asked me to put my phone next to the dryer so he could hear the noise. I actually laughed because I couldn't believe he was asking me to do something so absurd. Even so, I tried to replicate the problem, but he couldn't hear the noise. Then he told me he needed to hear the problem before he could send a technician.

Frustrated after I ended the call, I immediately drove to the local store where I had purchased the units to try to get a resolution. Walking inside the store, I looked for someone in the appliances department, which took some time. I finally found someone, but he was assisting another client, so I waited probably half an hour because he was the only person helping customers in the appliance department. As I patiently waited for my turn, I walked around to look for the washer and dryer I had bought—and guess what? I found there was a recall on my washer. The recall included 34 models, approximately 2.8 million units. The manufacturer had received 733 reports of washing machines experiencing excessive vibration or the top becoming detach from the washing machine, causing serious injuries (Consumer Product Safety Commission, 2016). I felt I had made a bad decision purchasing these appliances.

When it was my turn, I asked for the employee's help. I told him that I had tried to get my dryer fixed, but the manufacturer refused to send a technician. He mentioned that he had heard of customers having this issue before, so he was going to talk to his manager and give me a call back. Four or five days later, I heard from the store. The person who called me was a manager, and she was checking whether I had heard from the manufacturer, which I had not. She asked me to call her if I did not hear from them within a week. Later that week, I received a call from a local repair and service company who came to my house to repair the problem. The technician told me that the problem was caused by a defect in the dryer.

This true story exemplifies what happens when the customer is completely outside of the service-delivery model. You are probably wondering if I experienced more issues with my dryer, and the sad part is ... yes, I did. The grinding noise returned, and the unit sounded like something was stuck in the drum. So much for having a quiet drying experience! The noise was so loud that, when the manufacturer asked me to place my phone next to the dryer again, the representative was able to hear the noise this time. When the technician they sent arrived, he explained that the manufacturer was well aware of the issue I was experiencing with the dryer and that it was caused by using low-quality parts.

Later that week, I received a survey call from the manufacturer to evaluate my level of satisfaction with the service I received. Let's stop to analyze this effort by the manufacturer to measure customer satisfaction and the likelihood I would recommend their service to friends and family. Some of the questions sounded familiar because they were part of the widely used Net Promoter Score (NPS) survey. Gathering feedback is a regular practice by companies looking to measure and monitor overall customer satisfaction. Then, what is wrong with this effort? First, the manufacturer failed to acknowledge that the reason I had to call a technician to repair my dryer (and earlier my washer due to the recall) was because they used low-quality products. I bought the washer and dryer to safely and quietly clean my clothes while saving water and energy. In this case, the washer and dryer were the vehicles to fulfill my needs. The survey highlighted that the company was unaware of the issues I had experienced; from their end, they were just following up on a service call. This is another example that illustrates the absence of collaboration between all the actors involved in the service-delivery model.

How many customers will just give up trying to find an answer? As a customer, will you buy again from these companies (both manufacturer and appliance store)? When looking at this issue from a customer perspective, the service-delivery model lacks customer involvement and participation of other internal stakeholders.

There is merit in looking at service organizations with a customer lens.

The experiences I just related are supported by research. Most information systems are designed using a company-centric perspective, not necessarily focusing on how to create a unique and personalized interaction between the firm and the customer (Prahalad & Ramaswamy, 2004c). Technology is shifting from an enabler of business processes to a provider of the capability to achieve and maintain competitive advantage by facilitating service design, delivery, and influence (Orlikowski & Scott, 2015). Technology can facilitate and enhance co-creation of experiences by providing a flexible infrastructure where the organization and customer collaborate and co-create value together (Prahalad & Ramaswamy, 2004c). Customers have evolved from being passive to engaging in co-creation of value (Chae, 2014). Customers don't want to be spectators; instead, they want to engage and collaborate with your company. Firms can't continue to ignore customers when designing IT platforms. In fact, these platforms should be designed based on what is important to the customer.

That is why agile development methods have received so much attention, due to the central role of the customer in the development of services (Barlow et al., 2011). Agile methods have been recognized to facilitate value co-creation (Babb & Keith, 2011) for the ongoing effort of creation and transformation where service innovation is nurtured (Vargo et al., 2008). Agile methods rely heavily on face-to-face communication (Ramesh et al., 2012), but this arrangement has been challenged when development teams are not located in the same place. Implementation of agile practices with distributed teams poses several communication, control, and trust challenges (Ramesh et al., 2006; Ramesh et al., 2012). Maintaining the customer at the center when teams are not co-located is necessary for value co-creation. Understanding how value co-creation can be enabled by agile distributed methods (Corvera-Stimeling, 2015) could be extremely useful for companies who are looking to co-create value through all points of interaction between the company and its customers (Prahalad & Ramaswamy, 2004c).

# CHAPTER 4

~~~

## VALUE CO-CREATION AND THE ROLE IT PLAYS IN CUSTOMER EXPERIENCE

*"I have learned people will forget what you said, people will forget what you did, but people will never forget how you made them feel." – Maya Angelou*

Customer experience is a new topic of discussion for most organizations, but there are gaps in existing knowledge. Before we start talking about customer experience, we need to start talking about value co-creation. Value co-creation is a joint process through which the interactions of an organization and its customers aid the creation of value (Grönroos & Voima, 2013; Ramesh et al., 2012). The co-creation process allows companies to have a better understanding of their customers' needs, motivations, and actions (Prahalad & Ramaswamy, 2004b), which allows companies to move away from "best practices" and focus more on unique, personalized interactions between the firm and the customer (Prahalad & Ramaswamy, 2004b). Co-creating value with customers improves the overall quality of the product and customer satisfaction while minimizing the firm's risk (Agrawal & Rahman, 2015). It is important to emphasize that an organization has different stakeholders (internal and external) that are part of the value co-creation process (Ramaswamy & Gouillart, 2010). These external stakeholders include customers and third-party vendors. All these actors play an essential role in the value co-creation process.

In value co-creation, the customer is the only one that can determine value, and value is co-created when the firm is invited to be part of this process (Grönroos & Voima, 2013). An organization is only a value facilitator that provides the resources and processes to be used in the customer's value-creation process (Grönroos & Voima, 2013). At the same time, the customer alone creates value by using the services created by the company, but no value is co-created in this process (Grönroos & Voima, 2013).

It is important to highlight that the process of value creation is dynamic and is constantly evolving, based on past, present, and future customer experiences accumulated throughout the customer's value-creation process (Grönroos & Voima, 2013). Customer experience is part of the value-creation process, and only when the customer and firm work together is value co-created. This process is what drives innovation (Vargo et al., 2008). Therefore, customer experience forms part of the value co-creation process, but it should not be considered the end goal.

When firms design services without customer engagement, it is extremely difficult to fulfill customer needs, let alone exceed their expectations. Firms like yours often invest funds to grow and market your services without looking at the value co-creation process to understand how to better serve your customers to keep them engaged and eager to experience your services over and over again. Have you experienced and reviewed your services from a customer's perspective?

Interestingly, studies have found that improving customer retention is not necessarily a top business priority; in fact, it is ranked low (Jao, 2015). Firms are spending money to treat the symptoms, and the search for the solution to retain customers has become daunting for some of you. Few organizations can provide what customers expect not only now but also in the future. Do you understand why your customers are using your services? Do you know why your customers are leaving you? Are you providing services that your competition is not providing yet? Chances are, at least some of these questions remain unanswered. Many corporations are struggling to understand why customers are leaving them and why they are not attracting more clients.

At the beginning of December, I traveled to Atlanta for training, and my husband and I stayed at the hotel where the training was taking place. When we arrived at the hotel that night, we were tired from traveling all day. At the hotel, we registered and got our keys, but when we walked inside our room, we found it was not clean. The carpet was not even vacuumed. We were too tired to look for another hotel, so we decided to tough it out and started unpacking. When I turned on the bathroom lights, a clogged toilet with a floater greeted me.

We packed our bags and went downstairs. When we explained our problem to the front desk, the receptionist did not even apologize. She just gave us another room. The first thing we did when we walked inside our new room was to inspect the bathroom, where we found the toilet was dirty. Actually, it was more than dirty—it had feces around the bowl. By that point, I just couldn't believe our experience. We called the front desk and asked to speak with a manager. The manager apologized and said she was going to call her housekeeping manager to give us the keys of our new room after inspecting it. After we waited approximately twenty minutes, the housekeeping manager finally arrived. He simply gave us the keys to the room and left.

Do you think this hotel understands how to fulfill customer needs? If your company can't deliver the value your customer expects from the time the customer begins searching for hotels until the customer leaves your property, it is going to be particularly difficult for you to become relevant for your customers.

A lack of understanding about how value is co-created leaves companies in a fragile position. Focusing their resources on improving a fragmented portion of their service delivery will not improve their service. You cannot treat the problem by taking the portion that is not working and fixing only that segment without understanding the complete value co-creation process from the ever-evolving customer perspective. Fulfilling buying habits is not how companies innovate, and it is not how we meet current and future customer needs. Buying experience is part of the value co-creation process, but it is not the single factor needed to retain customers. Only when the customer and the firm collaborate can value be co-created. Value co-creation cannot exist without constant collaboration between the firm, customers, and third-party vendors. An organization cannot deliver value by itself (Vargo & Lusch, 2004b, 2008). As I mentioned earlier, involving the customer once the service has been created is not value co-creation. This approach rarely provides the firm the understanding of customers' needs, motivations, and actions (Prahalad & Ramaswamy, 2004b). Without customer collaboration and engagement, customer retention becomes extremely challenging. Understanding customers' needs is a difficult process (Thomke & von Hippel, 2002), but without customer involvement it is extremely challenging to understand if your services are capable of improving the customer experience by streamlining service delivery (D'Emidio et al., 2014). How many of the new services, systems, and/or platforms your company has launched have improved your overall business acquisition and customer retention? Companies that integrate a value co-creation framework deliver two to four times more shareholder value than companies that do not leverage co-creation processes (Libert et al., 2015).

Companies are looking for solutions, as evidenced by the increase of jobs posted in the field of customer experience. When reading some of the job descriptions, it is easy to appreciate the lack of understanding that exists. Providing great customer experience goes deeper than just adding it as part of your company's goals without making the necessary changes to adopt a value co-creation framework that supports collaboration efforts across all actors involved in the service-delivery model. Many chief executive officers (CEOs) are removed from what their customers are experiencing on the front line (Upbin, 2011). Companies are struggling to identify what is needed to fulfill customer needs to better retain their customers. Their efforts seem to be extremely siloed, or they leave it to one department to solve their issues. It is becoming a requirement of success for companies to offer personalized customer interactions, which requires an infrastructure in which suppliers, partners, and customers work as an ecosystem (Prahalad & Ramaswamy, 2004c). Each of these players has a crucial role in the value co-creation process, and it is of great importance to understand these roles (Corvera-Stimeling, 2015; Ramaswamy & Gouillart, 2010). Fragmented efforts to co-create value will fail to achieve a unified view of the customer or to gain the crucial understanding to be able to fulfill their needs. The customer will struggle to find value in your services, and you will find it difficult to retain them. Adapting value co-creation processes is not an easy task. So, how can companies like yours navigate and succeed through this journey?

Over the next several chapters, I will review some of the problems companies like yours are experiencing. Recognizing some of the challenges is necessary to identify potential recommendations to help your company achieve value co-creation.

# CHAPTER 5

—⌇⌇—

## PROBLEMS ORGANIZATIONS EXPERIENCE WHEN TRYING TO FULFILL CUSTOMER NEEDS

*"Most people spend more time and energy going around problems than in trying to solve them." – Henry Ford*

The challenges service organizations experience when trying to fulfill and exceed customer expectations are vast and continuously evolving. From a customer perspective, organizations can be divided into three major categories: firms who listen to their customers, firms who hear their customers but don't know how to fix customers' issues, and firms who ignore their customers. I will cover each of these categories below. Please remember that, to address the issues organizations are facing, we need to change the lens through which we view customers. To better describe the difficulties firms like yours are experiencing, we will look at the firm's structure, processes, participants, and platforms involved in the service-delivery process. When evaluating these organizations as a customer, we can identify issues otherwise not obvious or even hidden by other problems that make it impossible for businesses to notice them, despite being blatantly obvious to your customers.

## FIRMS WHO LISTEN TO THEIR CUSTOMERS

Firms who listen to their customers are truly interested and vested in their customers. The structure of these organizations facilitates constant value co-creation, their structure and processes support collaboration between the organization and its customers, and all this is enabled by the service platform which assists in this collaboration and serves as the venue for service innovation (Lusch & Nambisan, 2015).

Finding service organizations that are looking to amaze their customers at every opportunity is becoming more difficult. These companies have a framework that allows them to respond quickly to changes based on customers' current and future needs. These firms understand the importance of creating value in conjunction with their customers. The overall goal for these firms goes beyond selling their services; it is about helping their customers improve their lives. Each organization of this type has been able to foster service innovation by co-creating value with their customers.

These companies are not perfect, but they are constantly looking to review and improve their structure, processes, and platforms that support value co-creation efforts. These companies fall outside the scope of this book, so I will move forward to describing our next category: firms who listen to their customers but don't know how to fix their customers' problems.

## FIRMS WHO HEAR THEIR CUSTOMERS BUT DON'T KNOW HOW TO FIX THE PROBLEMS

Companies who listen to their customers do so because they care, but they may become frustrated when they don't know how to fix their customers' difficulties. In this chapter, I am going to examine a few areas where problems may exist. One of the first problems your organization may be facing is the lack of consistency in your service delivery. You may have customers leaving you because they felt they did not receive any value from your firm or your services did not fulfill their needs. They may have felt that your service did not help them or that you did not understand their needs.

## LACK OF SERVICE CONSISTENCY

For some firms like yours, maintaining the same level of service has been extremely difficult. Every year, you may be allocating money to improve overall customer engagement and retention initiatives. You may decide to add new services, change marketing tactics, and add new department units to handle some of the customer complaints you are constantly receiving. You have been operating in a reactive mode, where you feel you are addressing problems that have already taken place. By doing so, you are fixing problems from the past, but you can't stay ahead to engage with your customers, let alone co-create value together. This problem is seen not only in mature service organizations, but also in newer firms.

You want your customers to keep coming back. Companies' frontline employees —employees who interact directly with customers—are the ones that facilitate value. Firms may engage with customers through different communication methods, such as face-to-face or through online, phone, email, and digital platforms. From the customer's seat, customers buy a service because they are looking for a solution to fulfill a specific need. They don't buy a service for the sake of buying it. Therefore, customers are looking at your company as the medium to fulfill their needs. If you can't deliver on that promise and you don't attempt to fix the problem when the customer contacts you, you are going down a rough path that will likely result in a loss of revenue for your company.

Let's talk about a small, authentic Italian restaurant located in Scottsdale, Arizona. When they first opened their doors, they offered not only authentic Italian pizza, but also an incredible experience hard to replicate in other restaurants. This restaurant made every customer feel like they were the only customer in that restaurant. The staff was properly trained, and they took the time to explain why their food was different—where the raw ingredients came from, food preparation processes, and so on. The oven was visible as soon as a customer walked through the door, and the staff even took the time to explain where the oven came from. The owner would sit down and welcome you to his restaurant, making sure to ask why you selected his restaurant. If you were celebrating a special occasion, the staff made your special celebration memorable. Beyond the personal interactions, the restaurant was always clean, including its restrooms. The ambiance assisted in creating the ultimate Italian dining experience. From the moment you walked inside this restaurant to the time you left, you felt you had just had dinner in a little Italian town.

If you were to experience any issues, the staff would apologize and make every effort to solve the problem before you left. If they couldn't, they made an extra effort to have you come back to make it up to you. At your next visit, the owner and staff would welcome you back as if you were family. They were always seeking out feedback, identifying things that needed to change by asking customers if the restaurant fulfilled their needs. If a suggestion was provided, it was implemented. When you returned, the staff would ask if the change was what you expected. The service consistency was the same.

Unfortunately, as they started growing and opening new locations, the experience I just described disappeared. This authentic Italian restaurant lost its uniqueness. Customers initially selected this restaurant because it offered an authentic Italian dining experience hard to replicate in other restaurants in Arizona. Customers felt special, and when they wanted to share a special moment with their friends, co-workers, or family, they knew this restaurant was the perfect place. They could rely on what this restaurant offered—a location to create memories based on the purpose of their visit. After enjoying great success, the owner moved the restaurant to a better location and opened three more sites throughout Phoenix. Unfortunately, this restaurant lost all the elements that made it unique. The personalized experience they used to deliver to their customers disappeared, and it became just another generic restaurant.

Lack of service consistency can also be observed when

third-party vendors, who are part of the service-delivery model, are not integrated into a firm's service model. I recently went through the journey of finding a new bed. I was looking for something that was eco-friendly and breathable, offered support based on my sleep position, and had zero-gravity options and a massage feature. After extensive research, I found the company that offered the best solution based on what I was looking for. I visited the company and met the sales manager, who was very knowledgeable and took the time to explain how this bed was going to fulfill all my needs. The sales manager explained the warranty for the mattress and bed frame, and I decided to buy both.

A month after I received the mattress and bed frame, the massage feature started making a noise like a rattlesnake. I contacted the vendor, who asked me to contact the manufacturer of the bed frame. I was surprised by their response. How could they simply hand the customer over to a third-party vendor? As a customer, I was surprised because I purchased the bed frame and mattress thinking the same company manufactured them. My receipt listed the company, not the manufacturer. I contacted the third-party vendor, and they sent a technician to check the issue. When the technician arrived, he did not even know the company I bought the bed from; in fact, he had never heard of them. As a customer, I got worried because I felt the company had lied. The customer expects consistency when they engage with a company. A lack of consistency throughout the process creates anxiety for the customer, who may think that they may not receive the service they were promised.

As a business owner or business decision-maker looking at your firm from a company perspective, it becomes extremely difficult to identify which part of your service-delivery process is destroying value for your customers. When you are not co-creating value with your customers, you are most likely not fulfilling your customers' needs. Becoming immune to identifying value-creation processes in your service-delivery model prevents your organization from delivering the same customer experience on a regular basis. Identifying why customers are leaving you, why they are not coming back, or why prospective clients are abandoning you becomes extremely difficult. If you are only facilitating value, it is impossible to assess whether you are providing the experience your customers expect. Customers aggregate all the interactions they have with your company over time.

The two previous examples I presented illustrate the negative impact lack of service consistency can have on organizations. If you think your company is special because of the product quality you offer, you need to rethink your strategy because customers are assessing your company based on the complete service-delivery model, not just the vehicle that distributes a service. Customers are not going to visit your Italian restaurant simply because you offer

Italian food. Your customers are evaluating the entire dining experience, and if any of the elements involved in creating the dining experience are missing, customers will most likely start searching for a new place that offers them the value you used to deliver to them. Assessing the customer experience with a business lens provides a totally different view than when using a customer lens.

Once you have adjusted your lens, it's time to look at who should be involved in the process.

## SERVICE DEVELOPMENT WITHOUT INVOLVEMENT OF KEY STAKEHOLDERS

Lacking customer understanding can be dangerous for your business. How many corporate initiatives are launched without any customer input? Some of you have implemented processes that make great business sense, but when you evaluate them from the customer's seat, these processes are not exactly what you expected. This is a costly business strategy in the long run. These strategies emphasize the company rather than the customer. In most cases, these actions put the customer in jeopardy. Firms like yours implement these new processes in connection with key performance indicators to measure the overall impact of these new actions. Some of these key performance indicators put the company's needs before the customer's wishes. For example, some organizations measure average handle time, or how long call center reps stay on the phone with a customer. From the company's perspective, measuring average handle time provides a financial measurement for the firm, but not for the customer. The customer most likely will need to call back or will get transferred to someone else, who is going to ask the same questions he or she just answered for the previous call rep. Companies who use these types of key performance indicators most likely implemented them because it made sense from a business standpoint. However, they failed to take care of the customers' needs.

Failure to involve frontline employees, who engage with your customers daily, will also negatively impact not only your customers, but also your employees' ability to engage and connect with them. Lack of stakeholder involvement impedes companies to co-create value with their customers, resulting in delivering bad experiences not only to your existing customers but also to your prospects. A recent study by American Express found that 60% of consumers abandoned a purchase or business transaction due to a poor customer experience (American Express, 2014). Using traditional metrics is not enough. Metrics need to be crafted to inspire cross-functional collaboration of all stakeholders involved in the service-delivery model (Allen et al., 2005), and they need to be constantly evolving to mirror the changing needs of the customer. IT innovations have changed how customers interact with companies. Self-service channels have allowed customers to become active participants in the service-delivery model, and they have transitioned from being part of the audience to center stage (Prahalad & Ramaswamy, 2000). Understanding how your customers derive value from different service channels offers your company critical insights to assess the importance of different service channels (Scherer et al., 2015). From a company perspective, self-service channels may offer companies more efficiencies than personal service channels. But, when you analyze this decision from the customer perspective, the decision to offer only one service channel does not necessarily improve the relationship with your customer in the long term (Scherer et al., 2015).

Making decisions without engaging key players that are part of the service-delivery model creates a volatile environment not only for frontline employees but also for customers. Two in five customers do not think businesses are paying attention to providing excellent customer experience (American Express, 2014). When customers think they have not received what the company promised, they become aggravated before they try to find a solution. These annoyed customers were not planning to spend their valuable time trying to find some resolution to their issue. These customers grow more irritated when they get lost in your voice response system. They don't know which option to choose, and they just want to talk to someone that can help them with their problem. Finally, a call center representative answers the call, and this person has the power to calm customers or irritate them even more. If you can solve the customer's problem, most likely the customer's perception about your company will change. A successful customer service experience will help customers feel better than they had earlier when they were experiencing a problem.

Failure to involve other key stakeholders (e.g., third-party vendors) in the firm's service-delivery model could be detrimental to companies' value-creation efforts. Recently, my husband and I were looking for commercial retail space in the city of Austin. We have purchased a franchise, and we were using one of the commercial realtors recommended by our franchisor. The commercial real estate company was supposedly a national real estate firm, vetted and approved by the franchisor. The vendor was believed to be the best in finding commercial retail space for this franchisor. They knew the type of retail space required to fulfill the franchise model. We paid the realtor a service and travel fee for them to come to Austin to show us some locations. The realtor drove us around, but none of the locations he showed us fit the franchisor requirements. We needed premier real estate to drive traffic to our business. We have done our research about these locations. The commercial realtor provided us with data that was older than what we had gathered, so we started debating about the quality of his assessment of the market. When we tried to cancel our contract, the commercial realtor did not want to sign a release, so we had to get our attorneys involved. We were surprised to find that this commercial realtor was not even licensed in the state of Texas. Of course by then, they did not have any arguments against releasing us from the contract we signed. The franchisor had failed to exercise due diligence in assessing whether their recommended third-party vendors were providing value to their customers. Third-party vendors are part of the service-delivery model, so they will either add value or destroy value to the company's service-delivery model.

Not involving essential actors in service delivery leads to dissatisfactory decisions and resource allocation (Bettencourt et al., 2014). Value depends on context, and companies alone cannot understand the context in which their customers assess their services based on how the company helps the customer get a job done (Bettencourt et al., 2014). Do you understand if your company is helping or aggravating your customers?

## RELUCTANT TO CHANGE

Several firms are reluctant to change their way of doing business to improve customer retention. As a service firm, you are seeing a financial impact due to the challenges in fulfilling customer needs. If you are closer to the customer, you have a better understanding of what your customers are telling you. However, if you are removed from the daily interaction with customers, other priorities may take precedence even if you hear about problems with your customers. Year after year, your firm has developed the overall strategy for the company. Even if there are conversations about improving overall customer satisfaction, the new strategy is implemented in the hope that the customer experience will improve somehow. Rarely is the customer experience taken as the focal point to a company's plan. Conversely, customer-focused CEOs tend to have an obsession with all the details that make up a memorable customer experience (Upbin, 2011). Outgoing Cisco CEO John Chambers predicted that 40% of companies would be dead in ten years if they did not change (Bort, 2015). Lack of customer focus is not only a problem mature companies face; in fact, startups are also vulnerable to failing to engage customers (Upbin, 2011).

For companies, it is extremely difficult to change. In most cases, firms do not know how to change, so it is easier to continue doing what they have always done. Some firms have resisted listening to their customers and have defended any potential change to fulfill customer needs. One of the most common mistakes companies make is to ignore the need to improve the ease of doing business from a customer's point of view. If we compare the 1995 Fortune 500 list with the 2015 Fortune 500 list, we see that 57% of the companies that appeared on the first list do not appeared in the later list (Murray, 2015). Failing to embrace change driven by customers' needs is not a sustainable strategy. You can't continue facilitating value without taking your customers' current and future needs into consideration. If you are not addressing their current needs, you are most likely not going to be able to fulfill their future needs. The time when a company had control of the service transaction is gone. If your customer is not finding value in your services, your customer is going to find another company that does create value with them. History has proven that you can be the company with the most market share at this moment, but in the next few years, you may not be relevant. When your customers do not find value in your services, they will find a replacement, even if the change is painful. Arrogant companies are becoming less relevant in these times, when customers expect transparency, empathy, and respect from the companies they do business.

When services are designed without customers' input, they are most likely going to fail to fulfill customers' needs. For years, a big retailer has offered home delivery service, but when I purchased from them, their service did not fulfill my needs. As a customer, I based my purchasing decision on the information the company provided that helped me determine the value for their service. The day the order was scheduled to arrive, I decided to check the status of the order. The company's website listed that it was scheduled to arrive that day, but when I reviewed the tracking information provided by the delivery company, it showed the order was scheduled to arrive two days after the original delivery date. During this time, I received no notifications from the retailer explaining the reason for the delay, and the retailer's website did not show any delay with my order.

It still showed the original delivery date. Finally, the order arrived, but the quantities I ordered were not correct and the packing job was dismal at its best. I purchased a service based on information I found of value. Not only that, but I received the order late—so why did I pay to rush the order? I wasted money on a service I did not receive. What's more, I wasted my time tracking the order directly through the delivery company because the information provided by the retail company's website was incorrect.

If senior leadership is not close to the customer, it is extremely difficult for them to understand the magnitude of the issue. This problem is even bigger for companies who have a very complex organizational structure because they are even farther removed from the customer. Even so, reluctance to change is a problem in companies of all sizes. Smaller firms who are having trouble meeting their customers' needs are led by few executives making decisions for their companies. If those executives are not willing to change, they cannot be forced to change their strategy based on what their customers need. Failing to change will cause small companies to deteriorate just like large ones.

Interestingly, only 37% of customers are willing to give companies a chance to make up a poor service experience. If these relatively lenient customers experience the same bad service two or three more times, their patience becomes scarce (American Express, 2014). Customers are not willing to sacrifice convenience, ease of doing business, and simplicity. Companies are struggling to adjust their current structure and platforms to integrate and leverage customer involvement. Every year, companies spend a significant part of their budgets on marketing and sales efforts in new customer-acquisition strategies. These efforts primarily focus on what the company needs, without focusing on what the customer wants.

As a customer, if you felt your service firm did not understand your needs and the service you received was not what you expected despite spending extra time providing them with feedback on what went wrong, why would you consider this company the next time you needed similar services?

## INTERNAL CHALLENGES

Internal challenges create barriers for organizations to improve their customer engagement. Companies operate in a reactive mode, and once they enter this vicious cycle, it is extremely hard for them to break away from it. Mature service organizations tend to experience even more challenges due to the ripple effect of their inefficiencies and silo structure, impacting the experience delivered to their clients. In most cases, internal challenges are not isolated to one department; most likely, several departments fight their own battles in this unbalanced environment. Failure to address internal challenges can become detrimental to the organization. Under these circumstances, it is difficult to fulfill customer needs and pay attention to the most important stakeholders of your corporation.

Three years ago, I was rushed to the hospital because I was experiencing a seizure. Doctors ran some tests and determined that it was safe for me to return home after they did not find anything wrong. Six hours later, I was back at the hospital due to another seizure episode. This time, doctors ran additional tests, including a computerized tomography (CT) scan. It was around 6 p.m. Arizona time, and radiology personnel told my husband that he could stay in the waiting room, but he needed to turn off the television and lights before he left. They also told him that he couldn't leave the radiology department because he was not going to be able to access radiology again. My husband patiently waited for more than an hour and a half, and he finally called the operator to find out why the CT scan was taking so long. They informed him that I had been back in my room for the last 40 minutes. Radiology personnel not only left knowing that a patient's family member was still in their waiting room, but they also forgot to notify him that his wife was back in her room.

When my husband returned to my room, he asked to speak with the hospital healthcare manager, and the manager acknowledged that the radiology personnel were new and in training. Radiology reception personnel were never to leave unaccompanied family in the waiting area, and they were supposed to verify no family member was left behind. Neither of these two processes was followed. Internal challenges failed these customers, who were experiencing an extremely stressful situation. The customers were left wondering whether what they had experienced was an isolated incident, or whether they were going to continue experiencing issues.

Customers don't care if you are facing problems with your distribution channel, or if your technology is outdated, or if your sales department is not hitting their sales plan, or if you are short on staff. Customers will rate your company based on the value you provided them and whether you fulfilled and hopefully exceeded their expectations. Firms in a reactive mode have failed to identify the real cause of their problem. They waste resources, leaving the company in a worse position at the end of the year than at the beginning.

If your company is experiencing this type of concern, change is necessary. The most important mission for your company is to identify the real problem and find the appropriate solution. Unfortunately, in some cases, even if the problem is identified, changes will be implemented without involving key stakeholders. If customers are not part of the value-creation process, solutions will be designed and implemented without their input. These solutions will fail to address customers' needs, and the firm will continue to experience retention problems because this firm's services are not providing what the customer needs. This is a vulnerable position to be in as a company because you are extremely susceptible to losing market share to your competition.

Internal challenges are vast and random. The customer has no voice under these circumstances, and it is particularly hard for the company to understand and measure the impact their strategies have on improving their overall growth and retention strategy. Finding a solution to firms' internal challenges is crucial and necessary for sustainability.

## MANAGEMENT PARALYZED BY DATA

According to recent figures, 40% of firms are struggling to integrate data across all service channels, primarily extracting and acting based on insights drawn from unstructured data (Horwitz, 2016). According to Forrester Research's 2015 Customer Experience Index benchmark study, more than 85% of companies want to improve their customer experience efforts, but only 27% are succeeding according to their customers (Horwitz, 2016). Transforming customer experience through customer data will require companies to be obsessed about their customers to innovate and differentiate themselves from their competition (Horwitz, 2016).

We live in a globally connected economy characterized by constant data generation. Significant data is generated from internal and external sources; in fact, there are five main data sources: large-scale enterprise systems such as customer relationship management (CRM) and enterprise resource planning (ERP); online social platforms (e.g. Facebook, Twitter, Weibo, WeChat); mobile devices; the Internet-of-Things (smart devices); and open data/public data (e.g. weather, traffic) (Baesens et al., 2016). For big data to enhance decision-making, it needs to add business value (Baesens et al., 2016). Companies need to know more about the customer than what transactional data provides; specifically, they need to understand the human element behind the data (Davenport et al., 2001). Data analytics alone are not enough. These analytics must be supported by tacit customer knowledge obtained through direct interactions between the company's key decision-makers and customers to understand how customers use the company's services (Davenport et al., 2001) and evaluate if these services are fulfilling customer expectations . In addition, it is necessary to improve data quality to avoid the 'garbage in, garbage out' (GIGO) phenomenon and to develop high value-added analytic models (Baesens et al., 2016).

There are two billion people using social media platforms such as Facebook, Twitter, Weibo, and WeChat, and close to five billion handsets worldwide (Baesens et al.,

2016). Companies cannot continue ignoring the importance of integrating internal and external data to their analytics initiatives. The leading obstacle for companies when adopting analytics is the lack of understanding of how to use analytics to improve business (LaValle et al., 2011) and fulfill customer needs. Firms like yours are overwhelmed when recognizing all the moving pieces required to engage with customers and create value together to achieve service innovation. If you have a customer lens when assessing internal processes and strategies that are deployed every year, you will start recognizing the huge gap that exists between what the company thinks the customer needs and what the customer really wants.

Data integration without the context to assess the broader customer experience negatively impacts the customer's perception of your company. Let me provide you with an example illustrating the impact that lack of context can have on a company's ability to understand everything about the customer. No customer wants to receive a survey email to evaluate service satisfaction when the customer has not even had an opportunity to experience the service. Earlier in this chapter, in the section on lack of service consistency, I presented the example about my experience purchasing my bed. Before my bed arrived, I received a survey from the company asking for my feedback about my overall experience with the bed. This is a perfect example of a lack of context in data analytics efforts. The premature survey created a missed opportunity for the company to receive valuable feedback from the customer, and it triggered some unnecessary frustration for the customer, who had not yet received the product.

Over the past 30 years, companies have tried to find a way to measure customer satisfaction. Some of these metrics include customer satisfaction (CSAT), the Net Promoter Score (NPS), and Customer Effort Score (CES). Customer satisfaction has become the most commonly used metric in companies' efforts to measure and manage customer loyalty (Keiningham et al., 2014). Unfortunately, customer satisfaction is not tied to financial performance (Keiningham et al., 2014). Actually, customer satisfaction scores have no relevance to stock market returns (Chemi, 2013). Customer-driven organizations do not settle for one metric that is assessed annually or semi-annually; instead, they link various data streams to get a more complete picture of customer behavior (Baesens et al., 2016). Understanding if your customer is likely to refer a friend or colleague does not help companies to evaluate if their services are fulfilling customer needs throughout the customer lifecycle. Companies cannot rely exclusively on metrics such as NPS to measure customer satisfaction because customers may be satisfied with your company, but they are not reporting how much money they are spending between you and your competitors (Keiningham et al., 2011). In addition, NPS has other problems, including that the questionnaire does not help companies understand why their customers assigned a certain score (Price, 2015).

Organizations need to create perceived value for customers; in return, customers will provide value through distinctive forms of engagement (Kumar & Reinartz, 2016). Companies tend to look at a static event of the customer's lifecycle, instead of the complete customer's value-creation process. Furthermore, customer experience cannot be delegated to one person; for example, hiring a new vice president of customer experience will not provide the holistic approach that is needed (Lancaster, 2014) to co-create value with your customers in an effort to innovate (Corvera-Stimeling, 2015).

Development of digital technology and platforms will continue to challenge organizations' capabilities and willingness to collaborate with customers. Customers will continue to drive when, how, and where they engage with organizations. If your firm is not co-creating value with customers, most likely your firm is not innovating. Digital platforms have provided a medium for customers to share their experiences with their companies. Even if your organization does not have an official digital presence, customers may have started an unofficial one for you, and other customers might be using it to determine if they want to do business with your firm. Customers have been ignored for so long and continue to be ignored—unless these companies change their ways of doing business, they will continue to struggle to grow and retain their customers.

## LACK OF KNOWLEDGE TO DETERMINE HOW TO ACT BASED ON CUSTOMERS' FEEDBACK

Frontline employees interact with your customers daily, and these employees are responsible for facilitating value. These employees are the face of your company, and they constantly receive feedback from customers on their experience with your firm. This interaction can take place face-to-face, over the phone, via chat or email, or through a digital platform. Data collected from these interactions is crucial for your organization. Neglecting to use this data can be detrimental to the future of your organization. Companies should focus their resources on integrating employee feedback in addition to customer feedback systems (Benjamin, 2016).

Customers complain to frontline employees because they care about your services. If your company does not have a process to capture their feedback and act on it, your customers' voices will never be heard, and your frontline employees will not have an opportunity to contribute to your customer retention efforts. Frontline employees have acquired valuable knowledge throughout their direct interactions with customers, and they can be an integral asset for the organization's innovation processes (Engen & Magnusson, 2015).

Technology has advanced at a rapid pace, and customers do not see lack of knowledge as an adequate reason for not responding to their feedback or fulfilling their needs. From a customer's perspective, not acting properly based on feedback creates distrust between your firm and the customer. There is a franchise restaurant I used to enjoy. I would normally visit this restaurant when I wanted something quick, healthy, and easy to get in and out. Unfortunately, my last visit was as bad as the way management addressed my concerns. I placed my dinner order, and when I tried to find a place to sit, there was no room—most tables had not been cleaned. The restaurant was not even full. When I finally found a clean table, I noticed that the person who had been picking up dirty plates brought my dinner. He was not wearing gloves, but his fingers were touching my food. I started to feel a little uncomfortable knowing that my food was not managed correctly. I went to get a drink, and the beverage machine was dirty. I could tell they had never maintained it or even cleaned it. By then, of course, I asked to speak with a manager, but the answer I got from my server was that the manager was busy cooking and couldn't come at the moment. So, I left without eating, and I have never been back. I decided to notify corporate about my experience, and I even documented my complaints with pictures. I wanted them to know the level of experience I got at this location because I wanted to give them an opportunity to fix the problem. Corporate management sent me a letter notifying me that the manager of this location was going to call me, and they included two free $10 gift cards. I was very disappointed to receive this answer because the company did not try to investigate my complaint. Instead, they sent me back to the manager that did not have time to speak with me. As a customer, I felt I had just wasted my time trying to help this company fix a serious problem at one of their locations. I have not visited this restaurant again.

## LACK OF SYSTEMS/PLATFORMS TO INTEGRATE TECHNOLOGY AND EMPOWER HUMAN INTERACTION

Customers don't look at all the steps necessary to deliver a specific service or the cumbersome processes companies need to take to answer customers' concerns. The rapid pace of technological innovation is one of the greatest challenges companies currently face (Murray, 2015). Companies with outdated systems do not have the technology necessary to provide an outstanding experience. Even so, technology alone is not the solution either. Companies should focus on investing in better platforms that facilitate overall value co-creation opportunities, instead of just focusing on bringing new technology that does not integrate the customers' needs throughout the service-delivery model. For mature organizations, it is extremely difficult to be agile and nimble. In most cases, they have several legacy systems that do not communicate between each other, which makes it difficult for these companies to meet customers' needs and almost impossible to exceed customers' expectations.

Not knowing where in the customer's journey cycle you failed to deliver your service promise will impede your attempts to fix the problem and retain your customer. I can't emphasize enough the risk companies face by not understanding their customers' experience journey. For example, I have a credit card that I obtained in Chicago at my local credit union bank ten years ago. Fast-forward to last year, when I changed address twice, and the replacement card got lost in the mail. I called the 1-800 number and requested a new card. I also asked to update my name on the card because my last name changed after I got married. The call rep told me that, before she could request a replacement, I needed to call the local credit union to update my name. Since I called after 6:00 p.m. Central Time, the bank was closed. The following day, I called the credit union bank in Chicago. To my surprise, the person who answered my call was not in the mode to help. So, after my short conversation with the representative, I went to their website to look for the form I needed to fill out, but I couldn't find it. Instead of calling them back, I decided to cancel my credit card a few months later because it was too complicated to do business with this bank. When I called to cancel, I was surprised to learn that my credit card had already been cancelled. I never received a call to notify me about the cancellation, nor did I receive a follow-up call about the replacement card they mailed that I never received. All these interactions are part of the overall customer service-delivery journey. If companies don't track these experiences, customers and potential prospects fall into an abyss that is difficult to identify. Having the ability to understand what is happening to your prospects and customers as they are engaging with your services provides you an opportunity to collaborate with them and create value together.

## LACK OF DATA

Not having data and processes in place to facilitate data collection puts you at a disadvantage in terms of assessing whether you are fulfilling customer needs. Service firms who have highly disjointed distribution systems lack the ability to track customer sentiment in relation to their overall experience with your services. Customers expect their problems to be resolved or at least explained. Customers expect real-time solutions for their issues. Digital platforms have provided customers with a venue to express good and bad customer experiences. More than 90% of your customers who are dissatisfied with your services are not going to reach out and tell you about it (Afshar, 2016; Marketing, 2006), but more than 50% will talk about their experience with someone else. Generally, 26% will tell friends and colleagues not to use a company after a bad experience, 23% percent will share their experience online, and 19% will complain via social media (NewVoiceMedia, 2016). Companies that are not monitoring what their customers are saying will find it impossible to know why more than 90% of customers who are dissatisfied with your services are leaving you. It is also important to highlight the negative impact lack of data has on both your current customers and your potential customers. For example, 78% of prospects have abandoned an intended purchase due to poor customer experience (HelpScout, 2012).

Some of your customers who are experiencing your services are invisible to your company. Let me explain. Say a customer wants to take his sons to a basketball game. The night they decided to go, tickets are sold out, so the father buys tickets through a third-party vendor. The father is considering buying season tickets, but he is not sure yet. He attends the game with his sons, but he is, unfortunately, not satisfied with the environment the arena provided to him and his sons. He brought his kids, but he had to leave because people around him were swearing and acting inappropriately. As a company, if you don't have any processes in place to provide your customers a way to express their concerns—that is, a platform to report these type of issues—you will probably never know something is wrong because this customer is imperceptible to your organization. Being proactive to fulfill customer needs is becoming a requirement in today's connected economy.

Not having processes in place to facilitate data collection to improve customer interactions at every point of the service-delivery model will impede your capability to fulfill or exceed customer expectations. The power of knowing will allow your company to learn and improve the overall interaction with your customers. Technology should be seen as an enabler to facilitate value co-creation; it should not be seen as an opportunity to remove humans from the interaction. Technology should empower human beings to achieve a greater degree of customer service (Robischon, 2017). If your company doesn't have a strategy in place that seeks to understand your customers' needs, you are in for a risky and bumpy business journey. Not knowing what your customers seek from your services is the worst enemy of any business decision-maker. Companies need to be in constant search for ways to improve collaboration with their customers in real time to better serve and retain them.

## FAILURE TO UNDERSTAND CUSTOMER NEEDS

One of the major problems for some service firms is the lack of understanding of their customers' needs. If your company is not interacting constantly with your customers, you most likely don't have a good understanding of your customers' needs and motivations. Failing to identify customer needs can be highly costly for your organization. Implementing new technology or new processes and bringing in new vendors without understanding the reason behind these changes can be counterproductive or simply a waste of money. When there is no plan in place to meet your customers' needs in every interaction, the results could be detrimental to your business. New technologies, platforms, and services will not fix the underlying problem of not understanding customer needs. For example, if your company is driven primarily by metrics, you might decide that it is important for your call center to measure how much time your call reps are spending with customers. Implementing metrics is fine if you understand whether and how these metrics will help your company meet and hopefully exceed customers' expectations. The problem with this type of measurement is the negative impact it has on your customer, who may not have their problem resolved or may be required to call back. Customers want their problems to be solved in a fast, pain-free manner. This is just a simple example of the potential risks of being blindsided by not involving your customer in the value co-creation process.

Research has shown that many companies avoid interacting with their customers to learn about them. If we know that more than 90% of customers do not complain when dissatisfied with their companies (Afshar, 2016; Marketing, 2006), why would 80% of customer service inquiries submitted on social media go unanswered (Morrison, 2013)? Customers who do not complain to the firm when dissatisfied with their services should be a top concern for management (Stephens & Gwinner, 1998). In the service industry, firms are measured by their performance and actions. When you provide bad service, you can't take that back—you can only try to fix it. You can't replace the experience a customer just had with your company. For this reason, not understanding customer needs in the service industry is extremely dangerous. Once the damage is done, it is only fixable, not replaceable. On average, 58% of customers are willing to give a company with which they have experienced problems a chance to make things right (American Express, 2014). However, if the customer is ignored and believes the company does not care about them, 68% will leave the company (MacDonald, 2017).

It is important to note that companies cannot continue to fail at understanding how customers realize value from your services. Decision-making in a silo manner will prove detrimental to companies' innovation abilities.

## LACK OF FOLLOW-UP

Service firms who design, implement, and execute services and support processes without any customer consideration are doing themselves and their customers a disservice. If the service-delivery model relies on third-party partners, not understanding if your customers' needs are being fulfilled not only by your company but also by your service-delivery partners is a costly assumption in the long run. Let me take you back to the example I provided about the company I purchased my bed from. As I mentioned, the massage feature started making noise like a rattlesnake. I contacted the bed company, who said that the easiest way to handle this problem was to contact the manufacturer. From a customer perspective, this was confusing. I contacted the company I bought the bed from, including the bed frame. I did not know a different company had manufactured the bed until that point. Looking at this issue from a customer's perspective, this firm is asking its customer to contact a different company to resolve a problem. In the eyes of the customer, she feels that the company should be involved in the process and stand behind their service promise. Did I mention I bought an extended 10-year warranty, too? It is very easy to hand off your customer to one of your vendors, in this case the manufacturing company of the bed frame, to solve the customer's problem. However, doing so makes the customer feel that the company is failing to stand behind its service. Is your company making the same mistake? As a company, you should feel the urgency to understand what happens to your customers after you hand them off to a third-party manufacturer. Is your customer happy with the service this vendor provided? Was the customer's problem solved? How can you assure your customer's problems have been resolved if you are not involved in the process?

Lack of follow-up is a costly mistake that companies make. Studies have found that 70% of customers leave a company because they feel companies don't care about them (MacDonald, 2017). Only a few companies follow up with their customers after they complain (MacDonald, 2017). Lack of follow-up is so common today that it does not receive the appropriate attention it deserves. Customers want to feel the company they do business with will stand behind their services and follow up to make sure all their concerns have been addressed. Looking at this problem from the customer's perspective gives companies a glimpse inside their service delivery that very few would feel proud of. Company follow-up gives customers assurance that the company cares about them and will be there in case something else goes wrong. Customers want to know that, even though they experienced a problem with this company, the company made every effort to fix the problem. Customers perceive lack of follow-up as lack of interest in making sure your customer is taken care of. They may even feel you are trying to hide from problems you know have existed for quite some time but that your company has not attempted to fix. There are several scenarios I could portray, but problems will always exist. Companies that create value in conjunction with their customers want to listen to these problems; in turn, they try to fix them, and they keep the customer involved throughout the process.

Unfortunately, lack of follow-up is present in every industry. Recently, I noticed that my annual checkup was coming up. Normally, the doctor's office contacts me to confirm my appointment, but this time it did not happen. When I called, the medical staff informed me that the doctor had left the practice. As a service provider, he failed to notify his customers about his departure, and he did not provide any additional guidance to make sure his patients knew whom to contact in case they needed help. Don't let your customers wonder if they are going to hear back from you. If your customer reached out to your company for help, they expect a response.

## LACK OF TRAINING

Frontline employees are the face of your firm and the ones responsible for facilitating the value your customer will experience with your services. Frontline managers are vital also in the accomplishment of key business indicators, such as customer experience, employee engagement, productivity, and overall business goals ("Frontline Managers: Are They Given the Leadership Tools to Succeed?," 2014). Frontline managers, who are responsible for training and coaching frontline employees to fulfill your customers' needs, for the most part do not receive appropriate training and are not empowered to make decisions that will allow them to become more productive (McGurk & Vinson, 2010). Less than 15% of a frontline manager's role is structured to facilitate coaching and developing their direct reports. Lack of training, tools, and development negatively impacts employee engagement, goal alignment, communication, innovation, teamwork, and customer service, to name a few ("Frontline Managers: Are They Given the Leadership Tools to Succeed?," 2014). If frontline managers are not equipped to train frontline employees, do you think your frontline employees are fulfilling your customers' needs?

In the last two months, I have visited the warehouse club store by my house at least eight times. I have noticed the lack of employee engagement from the time I arrive at the store until I leave. Let me describe a typical visit. When I arrive, the parking lot is full of carts parked at the end of every row. As I am walking all the way to the end to get a cart, the employees in charge of the carts are either talking among themselves or looking at their phones, instead of making sure there are enough carts for customers. When I walk inside the store, this lack of customer service is present everywhere. The checkout process is highly transactional, and rarely special or memorable. Frontline cashiers are usually talking to each other or with the employee helping them to load the cart. Managers supervising frontline employees are busy talking to each other or checking which frontline cashier needs to get a break. They rarely engage with the customer. As I walk past the customer service desk on my way out of the store, I observe the same behavior. There are several possible reasons for this behavior: lack of training, employees in incorrect roles, or simply a lack of understanding to facilitate better interactions with customers.

On one of these trips, I purchased some patio furniture. I looked for someone to help me load three heavy boxes, and the reaction I got was not pleasant. The employee acted as if I had interrupted him as he told me that the cart was going to be at the checkout area and left. I had other grocery items in my cart, so I paid for these items. Then I walked toward the end of the checkout area, where I noticed my patio furniture was. I waited for five minutes, but no manager came to check on us.

I asked one of the frontline cashiers how I should pay for the furniture, and she said, "You need to talk to a manager." Then she left.

I couldn't believe it, so I walked toward a manager, who was talking to another manager, totally oblivious of what was happening around them. After I got his attention, I finally was able to pay for my furniture and left. In these situations, the customer is invisible to frontline employees and managers. These employees are not paying attention to their customers' needs. Companies are not looking at the experience they are delivering from a customer lens. The customer engagement offered by your frontline employees and managers can help you to create or destroy value for your company. If customers do not perceive value in your services, they will find alternative solutions to obtain the value they need from this interaction.

Let me to go back to the restaurant industry. Imagine you walk into the restaurant and, instead of welcoming you, the hostess says, "How many?" Once you are seated, the server takes your food order. Eventually, it arrives, and you eat.

Before you leave, someone comes by your table and asks,

"How was everything?" This person did not introduce himself, so you don't know who he is or why he is asking you questions.

You quickly answer, "Everything is fine," just so he'll leave quickly. This effort by the frontline manager is a waste of time, and his lack of training is observed and experienced throughout this restaurant. There is a knowledge gap that exists between what the customer is experiencing and what the company thinks the customer needs.

Last week, I called my satellite television provider to cancel a free trial period of their movie channels. I called one week before the trial period was over because I wanted to make sure I was not charged for a service I didn't want. When I called the company's call center, the call rep told me that I needed to pay $10 for cancelling the "free trial" early. I couldn't understand why I needed to pay to cancel a free trial. The call rep transferred me to their customer loyalty unit. The customer loyalty rep tried to explain the logic behind the $10 charge. After twenty minutes, she told me that I had to call back because she was experiencing computer issues. I asked her to transfer me to another customer loyalty rep, but she told me that she was not allowed to do that. So, I called back. When I asked to be transferred to the customer loyalty unit, the call rep became irritated and rude without any reason. I asked to speak with her manager, and she just transferred me without saying anything. When the manager got on the phone, he immediately apologized and explained that he couldn't cancel the "free trial" before the due date. He asked me to call back. I just couldn't believe it.

Lack of proper training for frontline employees and managers plays a crucial role in this issue. Several service organizations like yours find themselves struggling to make a leap in improving customer retention.

## FIRMS WHO IGNORE THEIR CUSTOMERS

These organizations are not necessarily the audience for this book. As these companies are not looking to make any changes to better serve their customers. Their culture impedes them to make any changes to fulfill their customer needs as they display certain arrogance and sense of entitlement. Company transparency and accountability are almost non-existent, and this behavior is displayed by not standing behind their services. The customer is not part of their daily business operations; in some cases, these firms create obstacles for customers to reach them when they have problems with their services. For these companies, their customer is invisible, and they want to keep it this way. With the increase in technology, they are having trouble hiding their behavior. It is only a matter of time before some of these companies find it difficult to stay in business.

# CHAPTER 6

---

## Desired Outcomes

"Get closer than ever to your customers. So close that you tell them what they need well before they realize it themselves." – Steve Jobs

## Company

## Innovation

Companies want to stay ahead of their competition. They also want to create a competitive position to protect their market share. Service organizations that have been successful in service innovation tend to engage and collaborate with their customers to design services that improve overall customer experience and simplify service delivery (D'Emidio et al., 2014). For some service industries, achieving innovation has become challenging due to their fragmented systems and platforms (Rai & Sambamurthy, 2006). The semiconductor business has transformed the industry by inviting the customer to the innovation process, and this industry has grown to more than $15 billion (Thomke & von Hippel, 2002).

Companies sell a service (Bettencourt et al., 2014). Without involving the customer and other key stakeholders, it becomes impossible for firms to be successful at delivering what customers want now and will need in the future. Large-scale enterprises face several barriers when it comes to innovation, but the major hurdle is the companies' business culture (Doss, 2015). Innovation efforts inside these companies are separated from day-to-day operations (Doss, 2015). Delivering what the customer needs lies beyond the performance of an internally-focused bureaucracy (Denning, 2016). For these companies, transforming their old way of doing things has been difficult. If companies are unable to fulfill current and future customer needs, they are not only spending money acquiring new customers, but they are also losing money when customers leave them.

Companies want to be able to retain their customers and

provide them with the experience that they need. The larger and more mature the service organization, the larger and more challenging are the issues that need to be addressed. Many underestimate the power of having a clear understanding of what the customer needs.

## PREPARE TO RESPOND TO MARKET AND CUSTOMER CHANGES RAPIDLY

Companies need to be agile and nimble if they want to quickly respond to market and customer changes. Companies need to move away from saying, "We are a customer-driven organization," while continuing to conduct their business as a company-centric, top-down bureaucracy focused on delivering value to shareholders (Denning, 2016). Companies know they need to change and become passionately obsessed about the customer to accommodate customers' demands, but most don't know how. Corporations understand they must change, but they have not been able to do so, in part because their structure makes collaboration efforts with their customers extremely difficult to accomplish. Being able to respond to customer demands becomes highly challenging when internal priorities take precedence over changes necessary to fulfill customer needs. Not having a clear understanding of how to respond to market and customer changes will hamper the company's efforts to better position their company ahead of their competition and at the forefront of their customers' minds.

Companies who can improve their competitive position do so as a result of actions taken to improve the value provided to their customers, not the other way around. Businesses that are successful are better at positioning their company not only to provide a solution to customers' needs, but also to provide the best service and value to their customers.

## UNIFIED VIEW OF THE CUSTOMER ACROSS CHANNELS

Companies want to have a better understanding of the customers they service across multiple channels. Advances in technology and the Internet-of-Things have transformed the way companies interact with customers. Companies have seen a significant transition in their service-delivery model, going from a single channel to a multi-channel. The last few years have witnessed a surge in the business world as companies move from multi-channel to omni-channel. In an omni-channel environment, all channels are managed together, allowing companies to offer a holistic customer experience across channels (Juaneda-Ayensa et al., 2016). Having an omni-channel strategy helps customers to have a complete, unique, and seamless experience between channels (Juaneda-Ayensa et al., 2016). It is extremely important for companies to understand their customer needs so they can determine the right strategy for them. Companies should assess where their customers are before determining if an omni-channel strategy is the best option for them (Newman, 2015). Customers are interested only in having a seamless experience when engaging with your company. More than ever, customers are determining how they want to engage with companies. Companies need to understand how they are fulfilling customers' needs by channel and how they will accomplish that managing all channels as a whole. Integration of channels should be driven by enabling value co-creation between a company and its customers, and it should not be driven by technology alone. Instead, technology should be considered as the platform where value co-creation takes places, rather than as the solution.

If your service-delivery model involves third parties, understanding what happens after your customer interacts with your vendors should also be considered part of your unified view of the customer. Companies in general want to better serve their customers, they want to avoid complaints if possible, and they want to understand the journey their customers took to resolve a problem. Companies would love to change the conversation from "I *want*" to "I *can* better serve my customers because I have been able to identify what is causing my customers to leave me."

Consistency in the service industry is crucial and difficult to accomplish when services are heterogeneous by nature (Tatikonda & Zeithaml, 2002). Trying to ensure consistency across channels is even harder to accomplish. Understanding customers' needs will help companies in their journey to have a more unified view of the customer.

## IMPROVED CUSTOMER RETENTION

For the most part, service firms want to retain their customers. On average, it is 5 to 25 times more expensive to acquire a new customer than to retain an existing one (Gallo, 2014). A 5% increase in customer retention could result in a profit increase between 25% and 95% (Gallo, 2014). Companies that spend a deficient amount on customer retention will experience a greater impact on long-term customer profitability than if they engage in suboptimal acquisition spending (Reinartz et al., 2005). Value co-creation happens over time. The value perceived by customers and the firm need to be aligned throughout the continuous changes necessary to ensure fulfillment of customer needs and market competitiveness (Kumar & Reinartz, 2016). Customer retention problems due to poor customer experience are costing companies billions of dollars. Between the US, the UK, and Australia, bad service is costing companies $206 billion a year (Colson, 2017; Hyken, 2016; Writers, 2016). Understanding why customers are leaving companies every year should be considered a top priority in their agenda. Customer retention efforts tend to be reactive, and the root of the problem is rarely addressed. Being able to remain relevant should also be at the top of the priority list for most companies. Commitment to long-term success allows companies to avoid wasteful spending and lack of customer focus.

## EMPOWER EMPLOYEES TO DO THE RIGHT THING BY THE CUSTOMER

To create amazing customer experiences, you need empowered frontline employees (Bhattacharjee et al., 2016). Companies want to support their frontline employees to do the right thing every time they interact with customers. Companies want to empower employees not only to help customers solve a problem, but also to encourage truthful feedback and protect employees who answer honestly (Benjamin, 2016). Companies want their frontline managers to empower and train their frontline employees to help customers resolve their problems. Those who can do so experience higher customer retention rates than companies who cannot. Employees who are empowered are in a better position to engage and deliver value to customers (Kumar & Pansari, 2016).

## MAXIMIZE SHAREHOLDER VALUE

Public companies want to return value to their shareholders. Companies in the US and the UK tend to follow this direction, while France, Germany and Japan tend to advocate for balancing interests of all stakeholders (Mauboussin & Rappaport, 2016). In some cases, some corporations have focused on shareholder value at the expense of their customers. Having a short-term goal to achieve shareholder value to boost today's stock price is not the correct definition of maximizing shareholder value (Mauboussin & Rappaport, 2016). This interpretation of maximizing shareholder value will put the corporation in a very fragile state, where any unforeseen problem could take the firm off track. This approach puts the corporation into a reactive mode, where changes are implemented to solve the most immediate problem, even though this solution may impede the organization to achieve their long-term goals. Companies that manage only short-term goals to impact stock price do so to the detriment of their customers and eventually at the expense of the long-term shareholder. Their efforts are fragmented and isolated. The correct interpretation of maximizing shareholder value is allocating resources to maximize long-term cash flow and benefit not only shareholders but also customers, employees, suppliers, creditors, and communities (Mauboussin & Rappaport, 2016). Companies who have a clear understanding of the direction based on what their customer needs can improve shareholder value by fulfilling customer needs.

# CUSTOMER

## EASY-TO-DO-BUSINESS-WITH COMPANIES

In today's connected economy, people don't have time to waste on trying to contact a company to answer a question or solve a problem. Providing a superior and low-effort experience across the company's service-delivery model positively increases revenue growth 10% to 15% (Morgan, 2015). Customers look for solutions when purchasing a service. Corporations who can engage with their customers and work toward finding what the customer needs now and will need in the future are better equipped to co-create value with their customers. Companies can foster innovation through value co-creation (Corvera-Stimeling, 2015). One of the most common mistakes companies make is not having a clear understanding of how customers use a specific service to fulfill their specific need. A recent poll reported that 84% of global executives believe innovation is a priority for their growth strategies, but only 6% were satisfied with their companies' innovation efforts (Christensen et al., 2016). Anticipating current and future customer needs is a necessity for companies to stay relevant.

Each customer's interpretation of ease of doing business is different, but in general it can be defined as assisting your customers to find solutions to meet their needs or problems. Customers expect to have a quick, simple encounter every time they engage with your firm. Nowadays, firms that understand their potential customers' needs are better prepared to engage with their customers.

Every time the customer engages with your company, your customer is assessing these interactions. Your customer's view of your company is the sum of all these interactions. Customers will remember bad experiences and how you made them feel. If the experience is extremely painful for your customer, your company most likely is going to lose this customer. Customers will tell eight people about their good experience and over twice as many people about their poor experience (American Express, 2014). A full 60% of customers who have a bad customer experience with a company will not do business with them again (American Express, 2014).

When customers interact with companies, they pay attention to what is important to them. They want to get a satisfactory answer to their question and interact with someone who is knowledgeable, makes them feel they are important to the company, and provides a personalized experience with follow-up (American Express, 2014). If a company provides a customer with their best-ever experience, that customer will compare this experience with every single experience they have with companies in the future. Let me give you an example. Imagine you are visiting a hotel for business, and you choose one that primarily targets customers who value feeling as close as possible to home. They offer an open floor plan, a comfortable bed, a place to hang clothes and coats without touching the carpet, extremely clean bedrooms, water, and coffee. Before you arrive at this hotel, you receive an email asking if you would like to make any special requests to make sure your stay is as comfortable as possible.

I visited this hotel on my last trip to Las Vegas. I was looking for a hotel that would offer me all the elements I described above. I arrived at the hotel after a long travel day. A valet greeted me and gave me a ticket for my luggage. I was personally walked to the front desk while the valet removed my luggage from my car. As soon as I checked in at the front desk, the staff welcomed me to the hotel. They checked me in and highlighted the fact that the water and coffee I requested were waiting in my room. They even said that, if I needed more, I should please just call. In regard to my food allergies, they mentioned that they had already notified the chef, in case I needed to order any food. The front desk gave my room keys to the bellman, and they walked with me to show me my room. As soon as we arrived at my room, he made sure I had water and coffee, like I requested, and he asked me if there was anything else I needed. The room was immaculate. I could tell they actually cleaned and vacuumed it. The closets were clean, and the TV remote had a protective cover, letting me know that the remote had been disinfected. After I settled in my room, I ordered dinner, and they made dinner recommendations based on my food allergies.

As a customer, this hotel provided more than I was expecting. Every single interaction I had with the staff at this hotel was impressive, and this level of service continued throughout my stay. When I checked out, the front-desk rep asked very specific questions about my stay to make sure it was pleasant. By the time I got home that night, I had already received an email thanking me for staying at this hotel and asking if there was anything they could have done differently to improve my experience. What is the likelihood that, as a customer, I will stay at a different hotel when I visit Las Vegas or other cities where they have a hotel? As a customer, I will probably try to stay at this hotel every time.

For a customer who enjoys this experience, this hotel will serve as the standard anytime the customer considers other hotels. The customer will compare the level of service she had at this hotel with other service firms she engages with. It doesn't matter if these companies are not in the hotel industry; this customer will use this experience as the base to measure airlines, restaurants, sports arenas, retail stores, cable companies, and Internet and technology providers. When a company establishes excellence in service delivery, this new standard becomes the standard the customer will use to assess other firm engagements. As a firm, not understanding your customer needs becomes a dangerous mistake because you don't have the knowledge required to address customer retention issues. It is only a matter of time before you start the vicious reactive cycle, where you are trying to fix what you thought was the problem without addressing the root cause of the problem. This mistake is extremely costly.

## MAKE MY LIFE EASIER AND LET ME HAVE CONTROL OVER THE INTERACTION

Customers want to have options in how they communicate with companies. Customers don't want to be forced to use one communication channel. Instead, they want to be able to select which is convenient based on their specific needs at a specific time. Offering a balance between self-service and personal service is associated with the lowest probability of customer defection (Scherer et al., 2015). The power of actively managing value co-creation gives companies better understanding of what channels provide a better customer experience (Scherer et al., 2015). Simplifying the life of a customer is highly desirable. Recently, 59% of customers reported spending more than an average effort to resolve an issue (Dixon et al., 2010). Consider a situation in which you are a customer who needs to get your windshield repaired. If you are busy and can't spend time talking or chatting with your service provider, you would most likely try to use a self-service application to set an appointment to replace your windshield without having to interrupt your schedule. Companies that do not offer different servicing platforms to help their customers have control over the interaction will struggle to fulfill their customers' needs. In this example, if calling a 1-800 number was the only option available to set up a windshield repair appointment, your busy customer likely would not have been able to set up an appointment to have someone repair the windshield. If you are this customer, you simply want to have control over your day and don't want to allocate extra time to deal with a problem. You want to solve it right away and forget about it.

For customers, having the flexibility to control how and when they interact with your service firm is becoming the new service standard. Even if the customer wants to control the engagement with the service firm, the customer will invite the service firm to participate if the company is providing something valuable that the customer does not know and was not able to obtain previously. For example, a customer may decide to open an account to buy stocks online. She wants to have control over her own research, and she does not want someone else managing her money. Due to her busy schedule, she wants to have the capability to access the platform at her convenience. At this point, she has done her preliminary research, and she has some questions she has not been able to answer, so she decides to talk to a financial rep. The call provides new information that assists her with her research.

In this case, the call was focused on this customer's needs rather than on the company's services. The financial rep offered to do some interactive training to guide this customer through some additional tools. The customer wanted to have control, but when the customer invited the service firm to be part of the value-creation process, the firm could take the lead in helping the customer meet her needs. The customer retained control but let the firm lead the experience because the firm was providing something of value to the customer. If the service firm stops serving the customer by allowing the firm's priorities to take precedence, the customer will take over the process and potentially end the engagement. Otherwise, the service firm will continue collaborating with the customer, and this value co-creation process will give the firm the opportunity to assess if the services the firm is providing are helpful to the customer. This is a crucial opportunity to identify potential gaps in the service-delivery process that need to be addressed to better service the customer. At this point, the customer has found this engagement extremely helpful and will continue to interact with the service firm based on her needs. The customer knows that the service firm is there for support. The customer still has the control over the engagement, and the service firm will continue to collaborate as long as they are still fulfilling the customer needs.

## TEACH ME

Firms that can facilitate learning as part of their service offering have a higher probability to engage with their customers. When you educate your clients, you are helping them value the benefit of your service as the solution to their needs. You must teach customers why they need your service before you try to sell it to them (Quinn, 2013). Your customers will find value if you are teaching them something they did not know before you engaged with them. For example, 58% of Americans have researched a service that they are considering purchasing online (PewResearchCenter, 2010). Customers are willing to spend time learning about your service if they see value in it.

Not long ago, I spent three months looking for a new vehicle. I knew I wanted a car that was safe and reliable, provided me with a comfortable drive for long trips, and had space for storage. I had done some research online and had identified three potential companies I decided to visit for a vehicle test drive. At the first dealership, I walked inside and was greeted by a salesperson who started talking about the specials they had that weekend. He just kept talking, never asking me what I wanted. The first dealer was not interested in understanding what I needed as a customer, and the salesperson did not provide any new interesting data to help me narrow my top three brands.

So, I decided to drive to the next dealership. I was starting to get a little impatient. When I walked into the second showroom, I was greeted by a salesperson who said, "I will be here if you need anything." He offered water and let us walk the showroom floor. They had only one sport-utility vehicle (SUV) on display, but this was the type of car I was looking for primarily as it met some of my needs. I climbed inside, but found that it did not feel that comfortable if I was looking to drive it for a long trip. I knew the company had some recalls recently on their SUVs, so I was uneasy about this brand. As such, I never called the sales rep to ask for additional details. Instead, I just walked out and decided to go to the last dealer on my list.

By that point, I was tired and not in the best mood to look for a potential SUV. My disposition improved when I walked into the last dealership, where a sales rep greeted me and asked me what I was looking for. He listened carefully to my answers and asked me more questions to clarify some of my points. He made sure the interaction was all about me. He was trying to understand my needs, even though we had not looked at any vehicles yet. He asked me to go to his office to show me additional information about the safety mechanisms in their SUVs, and he talked about what made their SUVs different from the competition. He told me about what made this specific SUV comfortable for long trips and how the SUV provided plenty of storage space. In addition, he talked about how the SUV was built and why it was the safer and more reliable vehicle. He even explained their service and maintenance program. Before he finished, he showed me some of their models I should avoid because they did not provide what I was looking for.

Finally, he mentioned two models I should test drive. I drove these two models and returned to his office. Despite his efforts, I was starving and was not in the mood to buy a car—and he sensed that. Instead of being annoyed, he told me I should grab some lunch and asked me to please let him know if I had any additional questions. He did not ask me if I wanted to buy the car, which was so refreshing. I didn't feel pressure, so I went to grab some lunch before driving back to the dealer.

When we walked inside the showroom, the sales rep greeted us with a smile, and we went back to his office. My husband was with me, so I told him that I would like to learn more about the purchase process. I also told him that my experience buying a car had not been pleasant. He said I shouldn't worry and that he would take care of everything. He provided me with additional information about warranties and repair costs, and he gave me some options to choose from. At that point, I allowed him to help me understand more about the life of the tires, maintenance, and overall safety of the car. Once I felt I had all the information I needed, I test drove the car and notified the salesperson to prepare the sale purchase agreements. My husband and I waited by the cafeteria, and when it was time to sign all the paperwork, we signed and drove back home in our new SUV.

Service firms who are focused on selling forget how the customer makes a purchase decision. The customer is buying a service to fulfill a need, and a customer who feels the service firm provides additional value will engage with the firm. The process of learning can take different paths based on the customer's needs. Being prepared to engage with the customer when the customer needs some additional guidance is crucial in the value-creation process. Only when the customer invites the company to collaborate in the decision process can the firm identify gaps in their service-delivery model and innovate.

## BEST CUSTOMER EXPERIENCE

Customer experience is predicted to be the primary basis for competition (McCall, 2016). Customers are spending money to find a solution to their particular need. They are not paying your service firm to waste their time or cause any discomfort by providing them with a bad experience. If you were looking to get away from your busy life and decided to spend some time by the ocean, you would want that experience to be unique, special, and all about you. You wouldn't want to spend time fixing problems because your room was not clean, your bed was not comfortable, the pool was dirty, or the restaurant was not willing to accommodate your special diet requirements. Do you get my point? You would want to make sure the experience was as rewarding as you envisioned it.

When I arranged for such a trip, the day of our departure finally arrived and we couldn't wait to have a margarita by the pool. We had selected our hotel and transportation after extensive online research and after calling the resort directly. The transportation company sent us information that would help us find them as soon as we arrived at our destination and maneuvered through all the distractions of the airport. We walked outside the airport to find people shouting at us, trying to sell their transportation and tour services. Since we had been warned about this, we knew what to do. We kept walking, just like our transportation company had advised.

We found the person holding the name of our

transportation company. She confirmed our reservation and introduced us to our driver. The driver introduced himself, explained where his car was parked, and helped us with our luggage. As soon as he got inside the car, he offered us some water and beer, which we gladly accepted. The car smelled fresh and looked super clean. The driver provided us with additional information about the ride to the hotel, explaining that we were going to go through some tolls, and he gave us an estimated arrival time. As customers, we felt comfortable and like our vacation had just started. Rather than engaging us in conversation, he simply turned on some music in the form of a nice Spanish guitar playlist, which helped to create the ambiance. As we sipped our drinks, we started asking him questions about the city, including some safety tips and where locals go to eat. Only then did he engage with us in a conversation.

As a customer, this transportation exceeded our expectations. This company knew how to make our experience unique, personal, and memorable. The thirty-minute ride to the hotel went quickly. Before we arrived at our hotel, he asked us at what time we wanted to be picked up for our flight back. We were not sure how many hours in advance we needed before our flight, so he offered some recommendations. Then we agreed to a time and signed a receipt. He assured us that our driver was going to be there at that specific time. The driver asked the hotel bellboys to help us with our luggage, making sure we were taken care of before he left.

We went to check in, and the person at the front desk was not as friendly as our driver. The interaction was very transactional. They offered margaritas while we waited, but it was clear the margaritas had been sitting out in the sun for a while because they were warm. They were not as refreshing as the beer we had on our way to the hotel. Instead of giving us our room key, the front desk staff handed the key to a sales rep who was selling time-shares. I told her we were not interested, but she would not take "no" for an answer. When she pressed, I told her just to give me my room keys, and she left. We felt we were wasting time. It was around 3:00 p.m., and all we wanted to do was eat some fish tacos and enjoy the beach. We did not want to buy a time-share, especially when we had just arrived and didn't know if we even liked the hotel, let alone liked it enough to consider buying a time-share. Finally, we arrived at our room, which was clean and nicely decorated with a beautiful ocean view. The bed appeared to be nice and firm, and the shower was a full-sized shower, with a tub in case we needed one.

We unpacked and changed before heading to one of the restaurants that served Mexican tacos. This restaurant had the most beautiful setting. We were sitting right next to the ocean, where we could hear the waves and feel the fresh breeze. Unfortunately, this beautiful setting was not enough to deliver the experience we were hoping to find. The service was bad. It took forever to get our food, and when it arrived, it was not what I expected. The quality of the food and drinks was low. We had been craving some authentic Mexican tacos, but what we got was not authentic and not even fresh.

Disappointed, we decided to leave and head to the pool. There, a very joyful young waiter asked us how we were doing. We told him about our bad experience at the Mexican restaurant, and he asked what we wanted with our fish tacos. Then he asked us how we wanted our taco meat prepared, and he told us that, from now on, we should just order any food we wanted through him. He would personally bring it to the pool or by the beach. He asked us what we wanted to drink, and we told him what we liked. From that point on, we did not have to ask him for anything. He would just surprise us with a drink that contained what we wanted. He spoiled us. Despite his imperfect English, he worked incredibly hard to make sure we got what we wanted. This hotel was an all-inclusive hotel, and he exceeded our expectations. This young man transformed our vacation experience from mediocre to the best we have had. He wasn't necessarily always working the pool we liked, but every morning he would look for us and explain our likes and dislikes to whoever was working the pool that day. This young waiter created our experience at this hotel. We never went back to the Mexican restaurant we visited on the first day.

Customers like me will aggregate all the experiences

they have with a company. Every person the customer engaged with will have an impact, positive or negative, on the overall experience. Location and ambiance must align with the service that is being delivered by all frontline employees. Service needs to appeal to your customers' emotions as well as all five of their senses: smell, sound, taste, touch, and sight. As a service firm, if you don't understand how your customers perceive your service and you are interested only in fulfilling corporate demands without understanding the impact that it has on your customers, you could be damaging your customer retention without knowing it.

## STAND BEHIND YOUR SERVICE

There is nothing more important for a customer than a company standing behind their service. In fact, 62% of customers reported having to repeatedly contact the company to resolve an issue (Dixon et al., 2010). Customers want the companies they do business with to be there when they need help or if they experience any problems with the services they provide. When customers complain, two out of three want some assurance that the problem will not happen again (Grainer et al., 2014). Since services are produced and consumed at the same time (Nijssen et al., 2006; Tatikonda & Zeithaml, 2002), if the performance of your company is not what your customer expected, the customer then expects you to try to understand the problem and find a potential solution. Customers are usually disposed to give companies a chance to fix a bad experience (American Express, 2014). Organizations who find a favorable solution for their customers are likely to do business with them again 70% of the time (HelpScout, 2012).

We know companies are going to make mistakes. However, you want to learn from your mistakes, so you do not continue repeating the same errors. Customers expect simple "common sense" solutions from the companies they do business with. Customers expect proactive behavior, honesty, and transparency. Customers don't like it when companies procrastinate to solve a problem.

Let's look at a recent online purchase I made. I normally buy my perfume at a local retail store, but between relocating, packing, and unpacking, I did not have time to stop at the store. I decided to go online and wait two days to receive it. When I received the package, I noticed the color of the bottle was different, as was the fragrance. I also noticed that the sprayer was bent, almost as if someone had tried to tamper with the bottle. I decided to wear it that day, but after thirty minutes, the fragrance was gone. I immediately realized that what I had received was an imitation or a fake version of my perfume. I called the online retailer. To my surprise, I learned that they had a policy stating that fragrance sales were final. Since this was the first time I had complained, they were going to make an exception. As a customer, I was a little concerned with this answer because I thought I was buying the original version of my perfume. I did a little bit of research and found that the online retailer had been experiencing fake merchandise issues for quite some time, but they had yet to fix the problem. As a result, I stopped buying from this online retailer. The services they provide no longer fulfill my needs. As a customer, having the certainty that the companies I do business with will stand behind their services is a must. My trust in this organization is now non-existent.

Customers want to make sure the companies they do business with have their best interest at heart. One of the top reasons customers don't trust companies is the lack of accountability in their services. Customers expect their needs to be filled every time you engage with them. If you can provide peace of mind to customers because they trust you and know you will be there if they experience a problem with your services, you are more likely to retain your customers. Standing behind your services will allow you to gain your customers' trust. This will allow you to invite them to be part of the value co-creation process, which will help you continue to innovate and exceed your customers' expectations.

Standing behind your services gives you as a firm an opportunity to interact with your customer and identify potential gaps in your customer service-delivery model. But, to use this opportunity to learn from your customer, you must first be ready to listen and help your customer.

## HELP ME FULFILL MY CURRENT AND FUTURE NEEDS AND REMEMBER I AM NOT JUST A NUMBER OR A LEAD

Customers primarily buy a service to fulfill their current and future needs. For service firms, understanding the current and future needs of their customers becomes one of the most important strategies to survive in an extremely competitive market. When a customer decides to select a specific company, there were specific solutions this company offered that satisfied the customer's needs at that specific time. A full 40% of customers will buy from a company that expresses an interest in them as an individual with distinctive preferences and needs (American Express, 2014). When customers travel, everyone has a specific need they are trying to fulfill. Customers understand weather delays and in some cases equipment problems, but they do not deal well with lack of information or knowledge. Customers may have planned their trip months ago, or it may have been a last-minute decision. Either way, if something is going to interrupt their plans, they want to know.

One afternoon, my sister notified me that my dad had passed away and I needed to get to Mexico the following day to be able to pay my respects before his cremation. I found a flight that afternoon that would allow me to be in Mexico the following morning, so I booked it. My flight had one stop in Dallas. The first flight was uneventful, but the second flight was not. The airline delayed the flight one hour, then two hours, then three hours, and this continued for more than five hours. Passengers had to wait eight hours and change gates three times, but the airline provided no information to calm their aggravated passengers. Without information, passengers could not assess their situation and determine their next steps. As a passenger, my needs were not fulfilled because I selected this specific flight because this was the only flight that would get me to my destination to attend my dad's funeral. Unfortunately, I missed his funeral, and the airline provided no apology for the delay.

As a customer, I know flight delays are going to happen. However, the way the problem is handled makes the difference in how customers assess their experience with their service provider. By not providing any information or guidance, passengers were not sure when and how they were going to get to their destination. Not understanding the customers' needs in a situation like this makes the experience even worse for their customers. Not having a clear understanding of their customers' needs at that moment turned this event into a volatile situation, where customers were so aggravated for not getting any information from the airline that the airport security was called as a precaution. During this ordeal, they promised on three different occasions that the situation was resolved. Each time, we found out that the gate they sent us to was not our final gate. Passengers had been waiting a long time and had been forced to move their luggage three times, only to find out each time was a false alarm. This airline did not meet current and future customer needs, and to this day, I will not fly them even if the alternative is more expensive.

Customers are patient if they are kept informed throughout the process. Understanding what the customer is going through is critical in the value-creation process. You can't deliver what the customer needs if you don't understand what the customer is going through. Companies who are running their organization from the inside rarely understand the impact internal strategies have on their customer. Are you fulfilling your customer needs? If not, are you alienating your customers instead of retaining them? Every industry needs to look at their performance through a customer lens.

For example, why is there such a knowledge and skill gap between what the companies need and what the universities are teaching students? Lack of co-creation in higher education is creating a lag between what businesses need and what universities are currently teaching. Collaboration between businesses and universities is necessary. In fact,

57% of business leaders and academics agree that collaboration is needed to effectively create value for students, academia, and businesses (King, 2015). Some universities have already started to move in this direction, allowing businesses, students, and academia to come together and develop the learning path to satisfy current and future needs while providing students the opportunity to incorporate experience-based learning into the program (King, 2015). Universities are also allowing students options to personalize the curriculum based on industry needs (King, 2015). Finding a solution to the gap described earlier requires all key players to collaborate in an effort to start the value co-creation process.

As a customer, if you are going to spend money, for example, in the sports service industry, you want your experience to be special every time you attend the game. If your experience is unique, you will probably look forward to the next game. The same applies to business customers, who may want to entertain their customers and create a memorable experience at your sports arena. As a service provider, every interaction is an opportunity to retain or lose a customer. Delivering the experience for your customers must integrate all the stakeholders involved in the service delivery as well as the platforms that support both service delivery and value co-creation opportunities. Sporting venues need to look at all the key actors involved in creating the experience for their customers. It goes beyond just attending the game and involves all the interactions the customer has before, during, and after the game.

## DON'T IGNORE ME

Customers expect the companies they do business with to be there when they need them. Customers want to find a resolution to their problem in their first interaction with the service firm. Customers don't like to be ignored. If they contact you, they have a question or a problem that needs to be solved. On average, only 1 in every 26 customers will voice their complaints (HelpScout, 2012). When customers decide to contact the company, companies ignore most of these requests. An average of 80% of inquiries go unanswered on social media (American Express, 2014; Morrison, 2013). A research study also reported that only 20% of customers who filed a complaint were satisfied with the result (Grainer et al., 2014). Additionally, 56% of customers who filed a complaint were ignored and reported that the company did "nothing" (Grainer et al., 2014). Some companies have forced their customers to jump through hoops to get any level of service—let alone provide an excellent experience.

As a customer, the last thing I want to do is waste my time trying to solve a problem with a service provider. If the customer is contacting you to get an answer or solve a problem, why not take this opportunity to create a pleasant experience for the customer? Recently, I had my annual physical and had some labs drawn at the doctor's office. A month later, I got a bill from the lab notifying me that my insurance denied the payment. I couldn't believe it, so I logged into my health insurance account and started a chat session with a representative. The customer service rep was extremely helpful and informative. He walked me through what he was doing, so I would not feel he had left the chat session. He checked the invoice I referenced, and he said that he was going to follow up with the lab company before following up with me. He asked me for my preferred contact method. Less than two hours later, he called me back and told me that they had sent the lab the information they needed. He also said that, if I received any additional correspondence from them, I should ignore it. I was quite impressed by the level of service this company displayed. He kept me informed throughout the chat session, and then they followed up with me like they said they would. All my questions were answered that day.

Unfortunately, not all interactions customers have with their service providers go as smoothly as the one I just described. Last year, my husband had two dental implants. The service provider helped us submit all the paperwork required to submit the claim to my dental insurance company. She then faxed the claim to the insurance company and sent me a receipt. Days went by, and I did not receive any notification from my insurance company confirming they had received my claim information.

When I called, they told me that they did not receive the paperwork. I thought that was strange, so I asked my service provider to fax it again. She even sent me proof that the fax went through. I called back, and they confirmed they had received all the information they needed. I looked online to see if the claim was processed, and they indicated that they needed more information. The good thing was that I was checking the status of the claim. If not, I would have never found out because I never received a call or an email to notify me that they needed more information. I called back, and they told me they needed additional information from the service provider. I asked them what information they needed and explained that the documents that had already been faxed twice included all the information they requested. They assured me that they were going to process the reimbursement. Another month went by, and I contacted them again, asking for a status update. For some reason, the claim was sent back because they needed additional information. To my surprise, it was the same information they had requested before. My service provider submitted it again, and finally I got paid. It took me approximately three months to get my reimbursement, and a lot of time wasted to get my claim processed.

As I mentioned earlier, customers don't like to be ignored. If they have to call several times to receive a service, they will eventually leave you. In fact, 37% of customers immediately consider switching to another company after encountering their first bad customer experience, and 58% will leave if they have two or three bad customer experiences (American Express, 2014).

How many times have you inquired about a new service by filling out a form on the service provider's website but never hear back from them? These prospects could become your potential customers, but if this is the level of attention you give them before they are your customers, why would they trust you as customers? How many customers have tried your services only once and have never come back? If the experience is not what the customer expected, 91% of customers will never come back (HelpScout, 2012).

## I AM STILL A HUMAN

Technology should not be used to remove people from the overall service interaction (Robischon, 2017). Instead, it should be used to improve the interaction and collaboration between customers and companies. A global survey which included 16 major economies indicated that, on average, 40% of customers want personalized service and they want their interactions across channels to be like a conversation (Genesys, 2009). Additionally, 86% of customers reported a high degree of interest to receive proactive engagement when they were experiencing issues on the Internet or self-service channel (Genesys, 2009). Customers also want better integration across channels, and they do not want to be asked twice for the same information (Genesys, 2009).

Last year, while living in Austin, I was craving true authentic Italian pizza. We had been looking for options, but we were not satisfied with the pizza restaurants we had chosen. One day, while driving on our way home after a long work day, we wanted to grab something quick and then go home. After an Internet search, I found a pizza place that had great reviews. We arrived at the location and were surprised to find it was a food truck. We met the owners, husband and wife, who thanked us for stopping by. The wife asked us if we had ever tried their pizza, and then she told their business story. They made everything fresh; even the actual truck and the oven were built by her husband. We ordered a pizza, and she gave us her business card in case we were unsatisfied with the quality of their pizza. Then she thanked us again for stopping by. We got home and tried their pizza, and it is probably the best pizza we have ever eaten. Days later, we visited them again. When we arrived, she remembered our names. In fact, as soon as we parked, she saw us coming and immediately welcomed us by our names. She asked us if we liked the pizza, and she was genuinely happy to see us again. This place became a weekly stop. Sometimes we would call ahead, and she was as nice on the phone as in person. She was truly genuine and thankful. We miss them now that we live in Arizona.

# CHAPTER 7

## BARRIERS THAT MUST BE ADDRESSED BEFORE A SOLUTION CAN BE REACHED

*"When you're finished changing, you're finished." – Benjamin Franklin*

Service companies who are looking to engage and collaborate with their customers to better understand their current and future customer needs could potentially face some tensions and challenges throughout this process. Service organizations that can adjust and tailor their services to what their customers want tend to have a service structure and service platform capable of managing the competing forces needed to co-create value with customers (Corvera-Stimeling, 2015). These competing forces will create tensions and challenges that need to be mitigated and addressed (Corvera-Stimeling, 2015). As a business leader, knowing some of the potential barriers you could face will give you a better understanding of how to prepare to address some of these tensions. Some of the tensions and challenges are reviewed below.

## COMMUNICATION TENSIONS

Having a structure that is flexible while preserving its integrity will create communication tensions. Structural flexibility helps your teams make quick adjustments based on changing customer needs, while structural integrity keeps key players united and connected (Lusch & Nambisan, 2015). Service firms who have developed silo structures over the years will experience even more communication barriers. One of requirements for agile development is to have face-to-face communication with your key players, but it is extremely difficult when your team and customers are distributed across different geographical regions.

Communication tensions will also arise as your key players may not be accustomed to the frequency, intensity, and type of engagement necessary under this new framework. Moving from a transactional to a collaborative communication style will create communication tensions. The pace at which change takes place also provides some communication tensions due to the formality required by players not involved in daily operations who normally will require formal updates as well as by team members immersed in the project (including the customer) who, due the rapid pace of development, need to interact informally.

## CONTROL TENSIONS

Service organizations will need to balance having informal processes and controls with maintaining formal controls to support the strategic direction of the company. The intricacies of the control tensions will surface due to the need to have structural flexibility while maintaining structural integrity. Control tensions will present themselves in various forms because of the dynamic environment required to foster value co-creation processes. Some of these control tensions could arise when partnering with customers from the beginning, instead of waiting for development and implementation documentation to be drafted before inviting the customer to be part of the process. Customer needs are constantly changing, which will create some tensions between the need to integrate evolving customer requirements and the need to meet delivery deadline expectations. Other potential control tensions could be experienced when the need for speed is of the essence for value co-creation processes, but internal processes (i.e., red tape) do not facilitate the nimbleness required.

## Team cohesion tensions

Collaboration among key players could become challenging when they are cognitively distant and don't share a common perspective. For service organizations to be able to co-create value with their customers when teams are not in a single location, they must reach a shared perspective and goals. Team cohesion tensions could also upsurge due to differences in knowledge and skills among team members, where collaboration is challenged by not having a common perspective. In today's environment, it is more common to have team members, customers, and third-party vendors not co-located, increasing the likelihood for the team to experience cohesion pressures. Achieving a mutual understanding of project requirements and priorities among all significant actors could create some pressures also. Team cohesiveness will be tested when some key players do not possess the knowledge and skills necessary to move at a rapid pace. Team members will need to rely on expertise coming from external partners, which requires the transfer of knowledge and skills. On some occasions, service firms may not be familiar with some of these external partners.

## Tensions due to technology versus customer orientation

Each participant that engages in the value co-creation process will have a different interpretation of the overall goal and output of their collaboration. What your development team wants and what your customer needs may be totally contradictory and conflicting. Understanding how key players come together and engage in the value co-creation process is crucial. Cooperation will be challenged if it is not possible to develop a united goal. It is extremely important to break down any disconnects and build a bridge to unite different perspectives to reach a universal goal if value co-creation processes will see any success.

## Challenges in designing the service platform

A service platform is the structure that supports the collaboration and value-creation opportunities between customers and actors, where resources and knowledge are shared and serves as the venue for service innovation (Lusch & Nambisan, 2015). There are embedded rules that govern how actors access resources; however, when these rules are not defined and clearly specified, integration becomes more challenging (Corvera-Stimeling, 2015). Incorporation of new technology under an aggressive timeline will also create challenges. Furthermore, the emergent nature of the technology as the project unfolds will create challenges throughout platform development (Corvera-Stimeling, 2015).

# CHAPTER 8

──◦◦◦──

## BALANCED PRACTICES TO HELP MITIGATE TENSIONS AND CHALLENGES

*"Innovation opportunities do not come with the tempest but with the rustling of the breeze."* – Peter Drucker

The practices presented below are recommendations for executives like you who are looking at ways to co-create value with your customers to foster service innovation within your organization. At the end of the day, you are looking to serve more customers and retain existing customers for a long time. I hope these practical suggestions assist you in these efforts. These practices will help you mitigate some of the tensions and challenges that you may experience when engaging with your key players, including your customers, so you can better understand and fulfill their needs.

## FORMAL STRUCTURE WITH FLEXIBILITY

The evolving change in customer needs requires companies to make rapid adjustments. The agile nature of this environment could demand team members to rely heavily on informal communication methods to facilitate collaboration among various players in the value co-creation process. Having formal channels to facilitate informal communication or interactions among team members can create efficiencies and avoid any delays. This practice allows firms to feel more comfortable having a structure within which informal communications could be channeled. A lead project manager could serve as the formal conduit where informal communications can be directed. Having a lead project manager that has a strong understanding of the entire project, including team roles and assignments, plays a crucial role in the overall success of the value co-creation process (Corvera-Stimeling, 2015). This person will manage the project timeline and provide guidance when needed based on their understanding of the overall project. The lead project manager will work closely with all players involved in the value co-creation process, including the customer.

In addition, having different levels of formality in terms

of documentation requirements can help to streamline processes, create efficiencies, and avoid some potential roadblocks. The level of documentation or formal approvals in a value co-creation process could constrain the level of flexibility required to move forward.

Collaboration between the customer and key players can be challenging when common understanding is not obtained. These players may possess different levels of understanding as well as different technical and business domain skills. Prototyping could help customers articulate their needs by allowing customers to better describe what they really want, and to experience and visualize the requirements and needs they previously articulated. Being able to fulfill customer needs requires a comprehensive and mutual understanding from all key players.

## CONSTANT COMMUNICATION

Constant communication is one of the most basic and forgotten elements needed to fulfill customer needs. For large and mature service organizations, collaboration is a complex task, due to their silo structure. Constant communication facilitates the creation of a unified, common goal. For some companies, developing channels that support constant communication will require them to adapt their processes and structures to achieve value co-creation. Constant communication assures team members, who may not be co-located or may have different knowledge and skills, move in the same direction and achieve a universal understanding of the overall goal as different interpretations will be clarified.

## TRUST BUT VERIFY

In general, mature service firms are not agile and nimble; therefore, fostering service innovation through value co-creation is quite challenging. Integration and collaboration are challenging due to their silo structure, and planning and executing projects could take years. Being able to accommodate alternative processes to support the agile nature of value co-creation processes is essential. These processes may require creating nimble procedures capable of avoiding any delays while assuring a standard structure is in place to protect and maintain any standard processes important for the organization. Trust will be developed between the customer and team members, but formal processes will need to be adopted to verify evolving customer requirements are being met.

## CUSTOMER INVOLVEMENT FROM BEGINNING OF INNOVATION PROCESS

Involving the customer from the beginning of the innovation process is necessary to engage in a value co-creation process that will allow you to fulfill customer needs and improve overall customer retention. If your service organization is waiting to obtain feedback at the end of the value-creation process, it is highly likely that customer needs will not be fulfilled. Interactions between all players involved in the value co-creation process need to be based on trust, transparency, and constant communication (Corvera-Stimeling, 2015).

## EXECUTIVE SUPPORT

Having executive support facilitates resource allocation and removal of any obstructions while adding accountability to all players involved in the value co-creation process. Executive support also allows full accountability not only from internal partners, but also from third-party vendors involved in the service-delivery model.

## TECHNOLOGY TO IMPROVE CUSTOMER EXPERIENCE

Investing in technology should be assessed not only as a way to integrate resources, but also as a way to improve the firm's customer experience (Corvera-Stimeling, 2015). When service firms can incorporate new technology as a way to co-create value with customers and, therefore, improve customer experience, they can continue to support innovation efforts, due to the results of customer involvement throughout this process (Corvera-Stimeling, 2015). Innovation efforts that do not fulfill customer needs will not be capable of improving the overall customer experience. These types of efforts are highly firm-centric and capable of improving only features of the service. They cannot support any value co-creation processes, which will result in an improved customer experience that will positively impact your customer retention.

## INNOVATION EFFORTS SHOULD NOT LAST INDEFINITELY

Embarking and fully supporting any innovation effort could be a daunting task. Research has shown that, by focusing on short-term goals, it is easier for these organizations to commit resources compared to a long-term commitment (Corvera-Stimeling, 2015). This does not mean that every short-term goal should not be completely aligned with long-term goals. If this is the case, organizations could fall into the trap of having innovation efforts that only improve service features but do not support customer retention efforts by improving the overall customer experience. Full collaboration from all strategic players is necessary to ensure the customer is at the center of the development process.

# CHAPTER 9

## CLOSING THOUGHTS

This book helps to bridge the gap existing in service organization literature and in practice. By understanding value co-creation and seeing how it can help an organization succeed, business decision-makers can begin the process of including customers in their innovation process. The recommendations I presented provide companies with additional guidance on how they can better serve and retain their customers. The service industry is the fastest-growing industry in the world, and businesses must engage in value co-creation with their customers to remain relevant. Customers will determine the value of your services, and obtaining their viewpoints is crucial to the success of your organization. *Voiceless Customer: Why Customers Leave* explains how to make the necessary changes that will allow an organization to thrive. In doing so, the book offers real-life examples to indicate where services break down and how businesses can avoid these pitfalls.

Through this book, I offered some clarity in regard to the topic of customer experience, which has gained popularity in recent years but is plagued by a huge knowledge gap. Customer experience is part of the value co-creation process, but it should not be the end goal. At the end of the day, firms are always looking to foster service innovation, and this could be accomplished through value co-creation. This book provides guidance on what is needed to improve customer retention through value co-creation. Providing a path to move forward through this journey was the primary goal of this book, and I hope that you have found it helpful. If you have any questions, or if you would like to continue the conversation, you can contact me through any of these methods:

| | |
|---|---|
| Email: | drfabstimeling@icloud.com |
| Twitter | @drfabstimeling |
| Website: | drfabstimeling.com |

# Acknowledgments

This book was inspired by organizations who have been able to co-create value with me as their customer. Their efforts to improve their service-delivery models have captivated my mind. The soul of this book was influenced by my research and by my fifteen years of international experience in all aspects of customer retention, customer experience, value co-creation, and service innovation. Since 2013, when the idea of this book came to light, I have been waiting for this day to arrive—the day I will be able to share this book with business decision-makers like you who want to co-create value with your customers.

There are so many people that made this book possible. I would like to thank my friends who encouraged me throughout this journey. I would like to thank my mentor, who helped me to keep in mind the audience of this book, in order to deliver something of value to them.

This book would never have been possible without the support of my husband. He challenged every thought and idea presented here. His strategic mind became invaluable in structuring the content to improve the book's flow. He spent countless nights and weekends by himself, while I was researching and writing this book.

# References

Afshar, Vala. (2016). 50 Important Customer Experience Stats for Business Leaders. Retrieved from http://www.huffingtonpost.com/vala-afshar/50-important-customer-exp_b_8295772.html

Agrawal, Amit Kumar, & Rahman, Zillur. (2015). Roles and Resource Contributions of Customers in Value Co-creation. *International Strategic Management Review, 3,* 144-160.

Allen, James, Reichheld, Frederick F., & Hamilton, Barney. (2005). The Three "Ds" of Customer Experience. *Working Knowledge* Retrieved from http://hbswk.hbs.edu/archive/5075.html

Allen, James, Reichheld, Frederick F., Hamilton, Barney, & Markey, Rob. (2015). Closing the Delivery Gap: Bain & Company.

American Express. (2014). 2014 Global Customer Service Barometer. Retrieved from http://about.americanexpress.com/news/docs/2014x/2014-Global-Customer-Service-Barometer-US.pdf

Babb, J, & Keith, Mark. (2011). Co-Creating Value in Systems Development: A Shift Towards Service-Dominant Logic. *AMCIS 2011 Proc–All Submissions. Paper,* 456.

Baesens, Bart, Bapna, Ravi, Marsden, James R., Vanthienen, Jan,

& Zhao, J. Leon. (2016). Transformational Issues of Big Data and Analytics in Networked Business. *MIS Quarterly, 40*(4), 807-818.

Barbera, Seon. (2015). Customer Experience Guide: What Millennials Expect in 2016. Retrieved from https://http://www.cgsinc.com/en/customer-experience-guide-millennials

Barlow, Jordan B, Giboney, Justin, Keith, Mark J, et al. (2011). Overview and Guidance on Agile Development in Large Organizations.

Benjamin, Beth. (2016). Listen to Your Employees, Not Just Your Customers. *Harvard Business Review Digital Articles,* 2-5.

Bettencourt, Lance A., Lusch, Robert F, & Vargo, Stephen L. (2014). A Service Lens on Value Creation: Marketing's Role in Achieving Strategic Advantage. *California Management Review, 57*(1).

Bhattacharjee, Dilip, Moreno, Jesus, & Ortega, Francisco. (2016). The Secret To Delighting Customers: Putting Employees First: McKinsey&Company.

Bitner, Mary Jo, Ostrom, Amy L., & Morgan, Felicia N. (2008). Service Blueprinting: A Practical Technique for Service Innovation. *California Management Review, 50*(3), 66-94.

Bort, Julie. (2015). Retiring Cisco CEO Delivers Dire Prediction: 40% of Companies will be Dead in 10 Years. *Business Insider.*

Cameron, Nadia. (2016). Report: Customer Service is Getting Worse, not Better. Retrieved from http://www.cmo.com.au/article/606918/report-customer-service-getting-worse-better/

Central Intelligence Agency. (n.d.). GDP – Composition, By Sector of Origin *The World Factbook.* Retrieved from

http://www.cia.gov/library/publications/the-world-factbook/
fields/2012.html

Chae, Bongsug. (2014). A Complexity Theory Approach to IT-
Enabled Services (IESs) and Service Innovation: Business
Analytics as an Illustration of IES. *Decision Support Systems, 57,*
1-10.

Chemi, Eric. (2013). Proof That It Pays to Be America's Most-Hated
Companies. *Bloomberg Businessweek, Dec, 17.*

Christensen, Clayton M., Hall, Taddy, Dillon, Karen, & Duncan,
David S. (2016). Know Your Customers' "Jobs to Be Done".
(cover story). *Harvard Business Review, 94*(9), 54-60.

Colson, Thomas. (2017). Bad Customer Service Costs UK
Companies Over £37 Billion a Year. *Business Insider.*

Consumer Product Safety Commission. (2016). Retrieved from
http://www.cpsc.gov/Recalls/2017/Samsung-Recalls-Top-Load-
Washing-Machines

Consumer Reports. (2015). The problem with Customer Service.
Retrieved from http://www.consumerreports.org/cro/magazine/
2015/07/the-problem-with-customer-service/index.htm

Corvera-Stimeling, Fabiola. (2015). IT-Enabled Service
Innovation—A Field Study of Agile Approaches to Value Co-
Creation.

D'Emidio, Tony, Dorton, David, & Duncan, Ewan. (2014). Service
Innovation in a Digital World. *McKinsey Quarterly*(4), 54-62.

Davenport, Thomas H, Harris, Jeanne G, & Kohli, Ajay K. (2001).
How Do They Know Their Customers So Well? *MIT Sloan
Management Review, 42*(2), 63.

Denning, Steve. (2016). Explaining Agile. *Forbes.*

Dixon, Matthew, Freeman, Karen, & Toman, Nicholas. (2010).

Stop Trying to Delight Your Customers. *Harvard Business Review, 88*(7/8), 116-122.

Doss, Henry. (2015). Why Big Business Fails At Innovation. *Forbes.*

Engen, Marit, & Magnusson, Peter. (2015). Exploring the Role of Front-Line Employees as Innovators. *Service Industries Journal, 35*(6), 303-324.

Frontline Managers: Are They Given the Leadership Tools to Succeed? (2014). *Harvard Business Review Analytic Services.* Retrieved from https://hbr.org/resources/pdfs/tools/Halogen_Report_June2014.pdf

Gallo, Amy. (2014). The Value of Keeping the Right Customers. *Harvard Business Review* (October), 29.

Genesys. (2009). The Cost of Poor Customer Service. Retrieved from http://www.ancoralearning.com.au/wp-content/uploads/2014/07/Genesys_Global_Survey09_screen.pdf

Grainer, Marc, Noble, Charles H., Bitner, Mary Jo, & Broetzmann, Scott M. (2014). What Unhappy Customers Want. *MIT Sloan Management Review, 55*(3), 31-35.

Grönroos, Christian, & Voima, Päivi. (2013). Critical Service Logic: Making Sense of Value Creation and Co-Creation. *Journal of the Academy of Marketing Science, 41*(2), 133-150.

HelpScout. (2012). *75* Customer Service Facts, Quotes & Statistics. Retrieved from https://http://www.helpscout.net/75-customer-service-facts-quotes-statistics/

Horwitz, Lauren. (2016). Companies Still Struggle to Unlock Customer Data Analytics Insight. Retrieved from http://searchcrm.techtarget.com/feature/Companies-still-struggle-to-unlock-customer-data-analytics-insight

Hyken, Shep. (2016, Aug 27, 2016). Bad Customer Service Costs Businesses Billions of Dollars. *Forbes.*

Jao, Jerry. (2015). Customer Retention Is King: The Future of Retention Marketing. *Entrepreneurs.* Retrieved from http://www.forbes.com/sites/jerryjao/2015/01/21/customer-retention-is-king-retention-marketing-provides-greater-roi/ – 37817b5c609a

Juaneda-Ayensa, Emma, Mosquera, Ana, & Sierra Murillo, Yolanda (2016). Omnichannel Customer Behavior: Key Drivers of Technology Acceptance and Use and Their Effects on Purchase Intention. *Frontiers in Psychology, Vol 7 (2016).*

Keiningham, Timothy, Aksoy, Lerzan, Buoye, Alexander, & Cooil, Bruce. (2011). Customer Loyalty isn't Enough. Grow Your Share of Wallet. *Harvard Business Review, 89(10), 29-31.*

Keiningham, Timothy, Gupta, Sunil, Aksoy, Lerzan, & Buoye, Alexander. (2014). The High Price of Customer Satisfaction. *MIT Sloan Management Review, 55(3), 37.*

King, Michael d. (2015). Why Higher Ed and Business Need to Work Together. *Harvard Business Review.*

Kumar, V., & Pansari, Anita. (2016). Competitive Advantage Through Engagement. *Journal of Marketing Research (JMR), 53(4), 497-514.*

Kumar, V., & Reinartz, Werner. (2016). Creating Enduring Customer Value. *Journal of Marketing, 80(6), 36-68.*

Lancaster, Mark. (2014). Customer Experience Should Not Be the Job of Just One Person. *Entrepreneur.*

LaValle, Steve, Lesser, Eric, Shockley, Rebecca, Hopkins, Michael S, & Kruschwitz, Nina. (2011). Big Data, Analytics and the Path from Insights to Value. *MIT sloan management review, 52(2), 21.*

Libert, Barry, Wind, Yoram, & Beck, Megan. (2015). What Apple, Lending Club, and AirBnB Know About Collaborating with Customers. *Harvard Business Review Digital Articles*, 2-7.

Lusch, Robert, & Nambisan, Satish. (2015). Service Innovation: A Service-Dominant Logic Perspective. *MIS Quarterly, 39(1)*, 155-176.

Lusch, Robert, Vargo, Stephen, & Tanniru, Mohan. (2010). Service, Value Networks and Learning. *Journal of the Academy of Marketing Science, 38(1)*, 19.

MacDonald, Steven. (2017). Why Customer Complaints Are Good For Your Business. Retrieved from http://www.superoffice.com/blog/customer-complaints-good-for-business/

Marketing. (2006). A Penny for your Thoughts: When Customers Don't Complain. *Research and Ideas*. Retrieved from https://research.wpcarey.asu.edu/a-penny-for-your-thoughts-when-customers-dont-complain/

Mauboussin, Michael J., & Rappaport, Alfred. (2016). Reclaiming the Idea of Shareholder Value. *Harvard Business Review Digital Articles*, 2-5.

McCall, Tom. (2016). Gartner Predicts a Customer Experience Battlefield. Retrieved from http://www.gartner.com/smarterwithgartner/test/

McGurk, Monica, & Vinson, Marc. (2010). How Companies Manage the Front Line Today: McKinsey Survey Results. Retrieved from http://www.mckinsey.com/business-functions/organization/our-insights/how-companies-manage-the-front-line-today-mckinsey-survey-results

Merlo, Omar, Eisingerich, Andreas B., & Auh, Seigyoung. (2014).

Why Customer Participation Matters. *MIT Sloan Management Review, 55*(2), 81-88.

Morgan, Blake. (2015). Want A Powerful Customer Experience? Make It Easy For The Customer. *Forbes.*

Morrison, Kimberlee. (2013). 80% of Customer Service Inquiries Go Unanswered on Social Media. *Digital.* Retrieved from http://www.adweek.com/digital/80-of-customer-service-inquiries-goes-unanswered-on-social-media/

Murray, Alan. (2015). 5 Things You Didn't Know About the Fortune 500. *Fortune.*

Newman, Daniel. (2015). Dreaming of Omni-Channel Domination? Start Here. *Forbes.*

NewVoiceMedia. (2016). Serial Switchers Strike Again. Retrieved from http://www.newvoicemedia.com/resources/whitepapers/serial-switchers-strikes-again-us

Nijssen, Edwin J., Hillebrand, Bas, Vermeulen, Patrick A. M., & Kemp, Ron G. M. (2006). Exploring Product and Service Innovation Similarities and Differences. *International Journal of Research in Marketing, 23*(3), 241-251.

Orlikowski, Wanda, & Scott, Susan V. (2015). The Algorithm and the Crowd: Considering the Materiality of Service Innovation.

PewResearchCenter. (2010). Online Product Research. Retrieved from http://www.pewinternet.org/2010/09/29/online-product-research-2/

Prahalad, C. K., & Ramaswamy, Venkat. (2004a). Co-creating unique value with customers. *Strategy & Leadership, 32*(3), 4-9.

Prahalad, C. K., & Ramaswamy, Venkat. (2004b). Co-Creation Experiences: The Next Practice in Value Creation. *Journal of Interactive Marketing (John Wiley & Sons), 18*(3), 5-14.

Prahalad, C. K., & Ramaswamy, Venkat. (2004c). The Future of Competition: Co-Creating Unique Value with Customers. *Harvard Business School Press, Boston, MA.*

Prahalad, C. K., & Ramaswamy, Venkatram. (2000). Co-Opting Customer Competence. *Harvard Business Review, 78*(1), 79-87.

Price, Bill. (2015). The Big Problems with Net Promoter Score: Do We Need A New "Ultimate Question"? Retrieved from http://labs.openviewpartners.com/big-problems-with-net-promoter-score/ – .WMsHcxiZMQ8

Quinn, Mark. (2013). Teach Customers Why They Need A Product Before Trying To Sell it To Them. Retrieved from http://www.businessinsider.com/how-brands-can-educate-customers-2013-4

Rai, Arun, & Sambamurthy, Vallabh. (2006). Editorial Notes–The Growth of Interest in Services Management: Opportunities for Information Systems Scholars. *Information Systems Research, 17*(4), 327-331.

Ramaswamy, Venkat, & Gouillart, Francis. (2010). Building the Co-Creative Enterprise. *Harvard Business Review, 88*(10), 100-109.

Ramesh, Balasubramaniam, Cao, Lan, Mohan, Kannan, & Xu, Peng. (2006). Can Distributed Software Development be Agile? *Communications of the ACM, 49*(10), 41-46.

Ramesh, Balasubramaniam, Mohan, Kannan, & Cao, Lan. (2012). Ambidexterity in Agile Distributed Development: An Empirical Investigation. *Information Systems Research, 23*(2), 323-339.

Reinartz, Werner, Thomas, Jacquelyn S., & Kumar, V. (2005). Balancing Acquisition and Retention Resources to Maximize Customer Profitability. *Journal of Marketing, 69*(1), 63-79.

Robischon, Noah. (2017). The Kings Of Customer Experience.

Retrieved from http://ezproxy.gsu.edu/login?url=http://search.ebscohost.com/login.aspx?direct=true&db=cph&AN=120412310&site=eds-live

Scherer, Anne, Wünderlich, Nancy V., & von Wangenheim, Florian. (2015). The Value of Self-Service: Long-Term Effects of Technology-Based Self-Service Usage on Customer Retention. *MIS Quarterly, 39*(1), 177-200.

Schettkat, Ronald, & Yocarini, Lara. (2006). The Shift to Services Employment: A Review of the Literature. *Structural Change and Economic Dynamics, 17*(2), 127-147.

Stephens, Nancy, & Gwinner, Kevin P. (1998). Why Don't Some People Complain? A Cognitive-Emotive Process Model of Consumer Complaint Behavior. *Journal of the Academy of Marketing Science, 26*(3), 172-189.

Swinscoe, Adrian. (2015). Is Customer Service Going To Get Worse Before It Gets Better? *Forbes.*

Tatikonda, Mohan V, & Zeithaml, Valarie A. (2002). Managing the New Service Development Process: Multi-Disciplinary Literature Synthesis and Directions for Future Research. *New directions in supply-chain management,* 200-233.

Thomke, Stefan, & von Hippel, Eric. (2002). Customers as Innovators: A New Way to Create Value. *Harvard Business Review, 80*(4), 74.

United States Census Bureau. (2015). *Millennials Outnumber Baby Boomers and Are Far More Diverse.* Retrieved from http://www.census.gov/newsroom/press-releases/2015/cb15-113.html.

Upbin, Bruce. (2011). Seven Signs of a Customer-Focused CEO. *Forbes.*

Vargo, Stephen L., & Lusch, Robert F. (2004a). Evolving to a New Dominant Logic for Marketing. *Journal of Marketing*, 68(1), 1-17.

Vargo, Stephen L., & Lusch, Robert F. (2004b). The Four Service Marketing Myths: Remnants of a Goods-Based, Manufacturing Model. *Journal of Service Research*, 6(4), 324-335.

Vargo, Stephen L., & Lusch, Robert F. (2008). Service-Dominant Logic: Continuing the Evolution. *Journal of the Academy of Marketing Science*, 36(1), 1-10.

Vargo, Stephen L., Maglio, Paul P., & Akaka, Melissa Archpru. (2008). On Value and Value Co-creation: A Service Systems and Service Logic Perspective. *European Management Journal*, 26(3), 145-152.

Ward, John. (2010). The Services Sector: How Best to Measure It? Retrieved from http://trade.gov/publications/ita-newsletter/1010/services-sector-how-best-to-measure-it.asp

Writers, Staff. (2016). Poor Customer Experience Costing Australian Businesses $122B A Year. Retrieved from https://which-50.com/poor-customer-experience-costing-australian-businesses-122b-year/

# INDEX

## D

## E

## F

# About the Author

Dr. Fabiola Corvera-Stimeling has more than fifteen years of international experience in all aspects of customer retention, customer experience, value co-creation, and service innovation. She has a proven track record helping Fortune 100 companies across industries with customer retention strategies when value creation is challenged by lack of collaboration and internal silo structures.

Dr. Corvera-Stimeling earned her Executive Doctorate in Business from Georgia State University, and her research expertise is in value co-creation, customer experience, and service innovation. She also earned her Masters of Business Administration in Marketing from Illinois Institute of Technology, and her Bachelors of Science in Electronics and Communications Systems from Monterrey Institute of Technology.

She currently resides in Phoenix, AZ with her husband.

For more information:

Email:       drfabstimeling@icloud.com
Twitter      @drfabstimeling
Website:     drfabstimeling.com